The Power of Words

Learning Vocabulary in Grades 4–9

Scott C. Greenwood

ROWMAN & LITTLEFIELD EDUCATION
A division of
ROWMAN & LITTLEFIELD PUBLISHERS, INC.
Lanham • New York • Toronto • Plymouth, UK

KH

Published by Rowman & Littlefield Education
A division of Rowman & Littlefield Publishers, Inc.
A wholly owned subsidary of The Rowman & Littlefield Publishing Group, Inc.
4501 Forbes Boulevard, Suite 200, Lanham, Maryland 20706
http://www.rowmaneducation.com

Estover Road, Plymouth PL6 7PY, United Kingdom

British Library Cataloguing in Publication Information Available

Library of Congress Cataloging-in-Publication Data

Greenwood, Scott C.
 The power of words : learning vocabulary in grades 4-9 / Scott C. Greenwood.
     p. cm.
 Includes bibliographical references and index.
 ISBN 978-1-60709-726-6 (cloth : alk. paper) — ISBN 978-1-60709-727-3 (pbk. : alk.
paper) — ISBN 978-1-60709-728-0 (electronic)
 1. Vocabulary—Study and teaching (Elementary) 2. Vocabulary—Study and teaching
(Middle school) 3. Word recognition—Study and teaching (Elementary) 4. Word
recognition—Study and teaching (Middle school) I. Title.

LB1574.5.G738 2010
 372.6'1—dc22   2010012722

∞ ™ The paper used in this publication meets the minimum requirements of American
National Standard for Information Sciences—Permanence of Paper for Printed Library
Materials, ANSI/NISO Z39.48-1992.

Printed in the United States of America

10/4/11

Contents

Figures

Acknowledgments

I am deeply indebted to many fine professionals who provided all kinds of support as I struggled with Parkinson's disease, making a challenging job even more difficult than I bargained for.

Tom Koerner, my editor at Rowman & Littlefield, is a delight to work for/with. He is a stickler, a realist, and a man who clearly knows his stuff! Additionally, I am deeply grateful to Melissa McNitt, my production editor, for crossing the Ts and dotting the Is and bringing this book to fruition.

Dr. Patrick McCabe of St. John's University copyedited with diligence.

Dr. Sharon Kletzien, professor emeritus and my former department chair at West Chester University, also lent her substantial editorial skills. She was somehow simultaneously brutally honest and encouraging.

Maureen Cook, a former graduate student at West Chester University, lent the invaluable perspective of a new teacher and potential reader.

Gina Evangelista, a West Chester University graduate student, gave substantive support throughout the entire process, particularly during the late (aka tedious, detail-filled) phases of getting the manuscript out the door.

Chapter One

Why This Book?

We are made to persist. That is how we find out who we are.

—Tobias Wolff

BACK-TO-SCHOOL NIGHT, FALL 2009

I am reminded of my own mortality as I record anecdotes about the literacy learning of my two sons, Nathaniel and Alex. I had them late in life, and I used to joke about how they'd be sending me off to the old folks' home at about the same time they'd be going off to college. My other one-liner regarded diapers: now I'm putting them on the boys; soon they'll be putting them on me. I am also reminded of how long it is taking me to write this book! Now my boys are 12 and 10 years of age, which fits nicely with the middle level scope.

Anyhow, regarding Back-to-School Night. The local school district is fairly large (thirteen thousand–plus students) and fast paced (over 90 percent of the high school graduates go on to four-year colleges). I dutifully follow the abbreviated schedule for my twelve-year-old. I attend Nathaniel's writing course, which is separated from his reading course. I believe that reading and writing are inseparable, but I don't want to come off as a complaining parent. What really, really troubles me, though, is "the list" of vocabulary words that are assigned on Mondays for the Friday tests. The teacher notes (proudly) that the students are supposed to use their new words in grammatically correct sentences every week. "I saw the aardvark" is grammatically correct, but it

1

offers no clue as to the writer's understanding of the word. The writing teacher has a master's degree and has been teaching for thirteen years. Does she know better? There's no surer way to teach kids to hate word work than the look it up—find a definition—use it in an original sentence "drill." My graduate students are well acquainted with the shortcomings of the "look it up" and "regurgitate it" methodologies. It doesn't help kids to retain new meanings!

Most teachers, whether required to or because it's important, focus time and effort on vocabulary work. Yes, the emphasis on test scores is a factor, but most teachers have goals that are larger and more altruistic than increasing standardized test results. Despite an increasing body of evidence about what constitutes "best practice," the fact remains that implementation of good vocabulary teaching remains elusive. Fisher and Frey (2007a) state, "Yes, we are flush with information about teaching students to read and write well. The challenge, it seems, is putting all of this information into practice" (p. 32).

Vocabulary breadth and depth develop rapidly from the early years through adulthood. It is estimated that children expand their vocabulary at the rate of about three thousand words per year—this equates, on average, to about eight new words each day. This phenomenal growth is largely due to the social use of language, formal and informal, with peers and adults. Additional and equally important factors are the child's intellectual curiosity and general maturation. Prior to learning to read, and when authentic communication purposes fuel their interactions, children integrate new word knowledge into their "bank" of known words. Then wide reading takes over as the primary source of new words.

Vocabulary knowledge has long been recognized as a critical correlate of successful reading comprehension. Many studies have shown that reading ability and vocabulary are related, but the *causal* link has not been demonstrated. Both vocabulary and comprehension depend upon the meaning of print, but at different levels—with vocabulary denoting individual words and comprehension involving much larger units. As children learn to read and gather experiential information (simply by virtue of more time living and interfacing with others, the various media, and print), their thinking broadens and they develop the tools to express novel conceptual relationships.

There exists, then, an ever-evolving recursive relationship between vocabulary knowledge and reading comprehension. It's also a chicken-egg proposition; wide readers may have strong vocabularies due to the fact that they read widely, or they may choose to read widely because they have strong vocabularies.

REGARDING SKILLS, STRATEGIES, AND ACTIVITIES

Teachers are often imprecise in the use of the terms "skills" and "strategies" as they relate to reading (Afflerbach, Pearson, & Paris, 2008). The general term "skill" was first used in the field of psychology. Reading skills have been taught for many years; more recently reading strategies have been popularized. One of the reasons for confusion is that strategies are used by teachers (to teach students) as well as by students (to construct meaning). Also, some strategies are used by both teachers and students. Thinking aloud, for example, is done by a teacher, as he makes his thought processes apparent. That same teacher might then teach his students to think aloud for the clarification of their own thought processes as well as their peers'.

Also problematic is the fact that skills and strategies may be overlapped, that is, used in tandem. Please be patient as the following discussion unfolds. When the teacher selects, say, the Frayer Model (see chapter 5), he is choosing a strategy and a structure for delivery to his students according to his purpose, lesson objectives, and time available. Same thing with concept circles (see chapter 4): he is choosing strategy and structure. *And* the requisite ability to map the letters to the sounds and meaning are due to the skills the reader has acquired.

Wait, there's more! This book will also offer a wide range of activities, which require learners to manipulate vocabulary for pleasure and enrichment. For now, make this delineation, and the nuances will be dealt with later. Strategies mean intentionality, are metacognitive, and require evaluation and perhaps revision. Skills are smaller, automatic, and rarely require much cognitive expenditure on the part of the learner. Activities are structures for practicing and reinforcing new and previously known vocabulary.

Interwoven in this chapter is a bit of the theoretical base for vocabulary study—keeping in mind that there is nothing more practical than a little bit of good theory. Then some time will be devoted to an examination of why "less-than-best" practices endure, despite evidence to the contrary regarding their efficacy. Please remember that the intention here is not to make anyone feel badly. It is important, however, to examine your practices and do what serves students' needs best. Do not lament past mistakes; rather, be reflective and honest to improve your instruction.

VOCABULARY INSTRUCTION: USUAL PRACTICES

Many teachers know vocabulary instruction is something they ought to be doing, but don't know much about it. They recognize that there is a need for it, but if they "do it" they often *assign* it rather than *teach* it. Unfortunately, in the absence of solid professional development, teachers often fall back to how they were taught vocabulary. Traditional vocabulary instruction is built on shifting sand: the erroneous assumption is that knowing a definition is the same thing as thoroughly and flexibly knowing a word's meaning. Many shortcomings of conventional vocabulary methodologies start with this assumption. The problem is exacerbated by the misuses of the dictionary, which is *not* designed to be a stand alone source of meaning. If a child doesn't know a word, "looking it up" is of negligible help. An articulated systems approach is called for. According to Fisher and Frey (2008a), "[W]hile there are exceptional and highly skilled teachers at every school, we are less sure about what it takes to ensure that all teachers have the knowledge, skills, and dispositions necessary to ensure that their students develop increasingly sophisticated understandings of literacy" (p. 32).

This is a book for content area instructors as well as English/reading/language arts teachers. It contains the hows and whys of good practice in working with words in grades 4 through 9. We need to clarify what is meant by "middle level." Middle level schools may be junior high schools (often including grades 7, 8, and 9) or middle schools (either grades 5 through 8 or 6 through 8). For the purposes of this book, the purview has been expanded to grades 4 through 9. Of course, many of the strategies and activities covered can be readily adapted to meet the needs of students below and beyond the chosen range—but our examples will stay in the fourth through ninth grade band.

Assigning Vocabulary Exercises

Here's the way it typically unfolds.

On Monday, teacher gives students (usually twenty) vocabulary words (possibly related to some unit of study, possibly not), sometimes with teacher-supplied definitions and sometimes not, in which case students look up a single definition in a dictionary. During the week, students memorize the definitions of the words, maybe using them in original sentences. On Friday, teacher gives a test on the targeted words, which students promptly forget as soon as the test is over. Some teachers give the students some choices, possibly allowing students to choose words that they don't know. Then, however, things get confounded by word recognition problems, and struggling readers with long lists of unrecognizable words get understandably discouraged.

These methods, their hybrids, and their adaptations are also pretty labor intensive for teachers, particularly when there is a lack of results. So, many teachers decide (or their administration decides for them!) that vocabulary workbooks are the answer. After all, they are teacher proof, easy to use, and consistent. Students don't even have to copy words, and teachers don't have to think too hard about what words to select; there they are—ten or fifteen or twenty words, neatly printed in columns, sometimes replete with single, short definitions and various "exercises" on the next few pages.

These exercises are often keyed to standardized tests. Preselected words are neatly presented. Real-world use of words, however, can be messy: it's not a multiple-choice world! At any rate, students do their exercises (synonyms, antonyms, etc.) to get ready for the Friday tests, again forgetting the words by Friday afternoon, but of course ready to start a new cycle of (usually twenty) words the following Monday. This requires a lot of work for the students (imagine figuring out "assuage" and "androgynous," when you can't even pronounce them, let alone tie them to your experiences), but not nearly as much work for the teacher. Yet any teacher who has "taught" this way knows how dreary it is.

It seems that more and more school districts are buying vocabulary packages to ensure consistency and articulation from one level to the next, rather than investing in professional development and deeper understanding of how to best teach meaningful vocabulary. It is probable that high-stakes testing pressures are a contributing factor. In the newly found interest in vocabulary testing, the reality is that the consumers are largely paying for articulated, consistent expenditures of valuable teaching time.

Definitional Approaches

Teachers are often frustrated when they ask students to use dictionaries to demonstrate they have learned word meanings. And middle schoolers are often frustrated when *they* are asked to look up a new word and are then (if they can find it readily) faced with a bewildering array of definitions to choose from, many of them possibly quite befuddling.

Put yourself in the shoes of an average fourth grader who is looking up "sinister" and finds "presaging trouble; ominous." Huh? How about a sixth grader who looks up "propaganda" and finds "material disseminated by the proselytizers of a doctrine"? Is the typical eleven-year-old patient enough to then look up "proselytizers" and extrapolate what's germane from "proselytize," a verb that means to "convert from one doctrine to another"? And then there's the word "doctrine" . . .

Going back to sinister, if that's an important word to know, a teacher might overlap *illustrating words* with a *definition* with a *hinkety pinkety* if he truly wants a child to retain the meaning of the word. What follows may look like overkill, but the overlapping strategies complement each other, thereby increasing the possibility of retention of the word's meaning.

What do you call an evil preacher? A sinister minister.
Have the students do a single sketch of an "evil" minister.
Then talk about the word "sinister"; the rhyme serves as a hook to help them
    remember.
Definition: evil, wicked

Another example, this time when older students encounter the word "smitten": What do you call a young cat that is madly in love? A smitten kitten. Hink pinks will be explored in more detail in chapter 9. Technically, hink pinks are one syllable pairs (e.g., polite rodents are nice mice). Hinky pinkys are two syllable rhymes (e.g., improved correspondence is a better letter). Here is one for you to ponder between chapters 1 and 9. It's a hinketyety pinketyety: Where does a New Yorker store alcohol? No peeking.

Quick anecdotes help enhance learning of words, coupled with examples. For "sinister," for example, advocate for a simpler definition than "presaging trouble; ominous." Sometimes less is more; just use the simplest word, in this case, "evil." Returning to the enterprise of traditional look it up–define it–use it in a sentence assignments, the middle schoolers write *a* definition (usually the shortest one they can find) and then learn to generate a generic sentence, because specific sentences can lead to trouble. So if the word to be looked up is "balmy" and the child uses/chooses "mild and pleasant," she might write, "I saw a balmy man." Consequently, the nuances of a rich word are not truly absorbed.

Do children actually learn more about word meanings by choosing among definitions for novel words? Probably not. Experience and attention to children leads to the belief that learning a definition is sometimes a good way to learn a word's meaning, but there needs to be more.

Definitions will be addressed in more detail in chapter 8, as you will delve deeply into more enlightened use of dictionaries. For now, just remember that definitions are contextually situated, that in the course of conversation we are more likely to give examples than full definitions. Definitions are "unnatural intelligent" acts. As children gradually refine their understandings of words, they learn characteristics that differentiate the key concept from another in the same category: say, someone who is *homeless* from a *migrant* from a *nomad* from a *vagrant*. Remember that the dictionary can be a valuable tool when used appropriately! Do keep in mind its limitations as well.

THE MATCH FOR MIDDLE LEVEL LEARNERS

FIRST DAY TEACHING IN THE MIDDLE

Tom Freed will never forget his first day as a teacher in a middle school! He was a secondary English–trained veteran who had spent ten years teaching high school students, and it was time for a change. His high school students often were just going through the motions, as many were more concerned with the exigencies of paying their automobile insurance than with Shakespeare or Hawthorne. They were pleasant enough, but Tom was concerned about his next twenty years and the prospect of growing complacent himself, of teaching one year twenty times. So he left his old district and moved to the position of seventh grade developmental reading teacher in a six–eight middle school.

The main thing that Tom remembers about the first day was the palpable excitement of the children, coupled with the noise level as they came charging down the hall. Some of them were dressed outlandishly. Tom remembers Heidi, twelve years old and in his advisory group, who later would write about "being trapped in a nineteen-year-old's body." Then there was Matt, who'd have sugary cereal at home in the morning, then stop at the local mini mart for a donut and a Big Gulp—he'd be screaming high for the beginning of school, then he'd crash by mid-third period (when he was in Tom's class, of course).

Symbolically, however, Mr. Freed's dearest memories are of Whitney and Shannon. Whitney was about five feet eleven and looked like a fashion model, a young Cindy Crawford. She was socially pseudo-sophisticated; her language skills were excellent, for she had been a ravenous reader throughout her years in school and at home. Her first self-selected book for class was more suitable for a college student.

Shannon, it turned out, was her best friend. He was over a foot shorter than Whitney, clearly prepubescent, and he had a little toy truck with him that first day that he "ran" on his thighs or on his desk, behind a little barricade of books so he would have his privacy. He was, however, gifted in mathematics. His choice for self-selection time was the Magic Tree House series.

Tom wasn't sure whether to be amused or aghast when he chaperoned his first middle school dance later that fall. The students seemed very childlike when they did the hokey pokey (what if that is what it is all about?), but when Shannon and Whitney danced slowly, swaying to the music, the juxtaposition of their bodies was not suitable for family viewing.

They were such an unlikely pair. But Tom soon discovered that he had entered "the range of the strange." Fortunately, Tom had a philosophy and a history of differentiating instruction. He felt that children construct meaning as opposed to extracting it. He soon came to recognize that he had been planted in the perfect venue for professional growth! Through graduate class work and attending conferences and workshops, he found out that there were unique characteristics of early adolescents, that things he saw and experienced with these children were normal, that things he did were actually best practice—in short, that he was not alone and was on the right track.

You, as teacher of middle grade students, have probably always had an interest in words, and have had at least an intuitive understanding of the connection between vocabulary breadth and depth and reading comprehension. It is never too late to learn about the developmental characteristics of "tweenagers." If you are at all like Tom and already have experience with middle level learners, you can probably relate to Shannon and Whitney when thinking about your own clients.

CHARACTERISTICS OF MIDDLE LEVEL LEARNERS

This section enumerates some activities to improve vocabulary instruction. Start with what you're doing right now, whether you are reading on your own, preparing for a course, or participating in a study group: read and reflect! You will learn to really tailor your vocabulary instruction, considering carefully the physical, social, emotional, and cognitive characteristics of this age group. Since this is a book on vocabulary instruction, the focus will be the characteristics most germane to word work.

Please remember, however, that vocabulary development is truly only useful and meaningful as words are applied to written expression (productive), oral conversation (again productive), reading comprehension (some would say receptive, but actually more productive than many think because a reader transacts with text), and listening comprehension (again, receptive and productive). Vocabulary work needs to be infused in a variety of ways for a variety of reasons. Teachers need to help early adolescents "get it" through careful scaffolding.

Socioemotional Development

Peers are extremely important to these children. A natural separation from parental influence occurs during these years, and peer friendships become critical. It therefore makes sense to have these students work cooperatively—

usually in pairs. This offers them the opportunity to talk more than if they work in larger groups. Another tenet to harness positive peer influences is displaying work. If a "cool" student creates some exemplary work for others to imitate or to adapt (better), then it is smart to capitalize on that influence. It makes sense to accommodate rather than to deny or squelch socialization needs.

Early adolescence is a time of identity development, and these children can be very emotional. A lot of the fluctuations are purely hormonal. Much of your vocabulary teaching should be centered on written communication (e.g., journaling, poetry) that allows and encourages the expression of feelings and emotions. These children are in transition and need practice in recognizing and processing changes that they are going through. Additionally, they need command of the "just right" words to convey what they are thinking and feeling. You will find that some of your seemingly shy and quiet students will thrive when given the opportunity to communicate in writing.

I'll share Meredith's poem:

Confusion

Who?
What?
Where?
When?
Why?
Questions
They are so befuddling,
Ringing in your mind,
Like a resonant telephone,
Just waiting to be answered.

Closely related to evolving identity development is middle schoolers' need for autonomy. It is the most crucial lesson a teacher can learn—we are all so afraid to give away control. Most of these children thrive when properly instructed as to how to be "turned loose." Learning contracts, for example, are tools that afford much of the requisite structured choice. Children do not automatically make good choices; they must be taught to do so. But the results of their word work when they choose and care are very pleasing.

Cognitive Development

Middle school students are "transitional" thinkers who are moving from concrete operations to formal operations. Put simply, they are moving from concrete/literal thinking, to being able to reflect and think abstractly—the heart of metacognition. Some children start making the transition at ten or eleven years of age, most somewhat later. The changes are gradual, and your students can shift back and forth between levels of operational thinking.

These intellectual changes go hand in hand with the socioemotional vicissitudes of this life stage. What's important from the teaching aspect is to recognize that children cannot be forced before they are "ready," but they can be helped along their developmental path with good instruction. Do you remember the riddle "What's black and white and 'read' all over?" Until they reach formal operations, they can't "get it" because of their inflexibility regarding red/read. These students are awakening to a world of imaginings and possibilities. As they become able to consider the feelings of others, they can "practice" word activities such as puns, analogies, riddles, poems, and metaphors.

Moral Development

Ironically, these middle school students can be predatory and unkind to their peers (because they want to draw attention away from themselves) at the same time they are deeply concerned about issues such as prejudice, war, hunger, and homelessness. Vocabulary can be connected to moral development in the sense that the right words at the right time are needed for cogent communication. Middle school students will thrive when they read books such as *To Kill a Mockingbird* (prejudice; Lee, 1960) and *Fly Away Home* (homelessness; Bunting, 1991), if you permit them to respond to works such as these in a variety of ways. Literature circles, for example, can provide a structure that elicits particularly thoughtful responses.

MIDDLE LEVEL LITERACY PROGRAMS

"Programs" should fit the needs of the students, not the other way around. Programs will be explained in this book not as packages, but as school-wide literacy philosophy and practice, as carried out in the content areas as well as the English language arts. Fisher and Frey (2008b) offer a five-step model for teaching vocabulary that is motivating and manageable for both teachers and students. This framework is grounded in current research and captured in these descriptors:

- intentional
- transparent
- usable

- personal
- a priority

Remember, reading "skill" does not always neatly "transfer" from one type of reading to the next. Students who are strong readers of narrative text in sixth grade may "hit the wall" in orchestrating the demands of seventh grade science text reading. This is often due to the conceptual load and the increasingly difficult vocabulary that is required for students to become "insiders" to the specialized knowledge of a particular content/discipline. Research has found that many students who exit their grade reading "on level" will not automatically become proficient "comprehenders" in later grades. They need to maintain and sharpen their skills through direct instruction and individual engagement with print.

That being said up front, here are some thoughts about middle level programming.

Encourage, Even Demand, Wide Reading In and Out of School

The connection between vocabulary volume and amount of independent reading done is abundantly clear. The best way to learn most words is through immersion in print. These students need to read a lot. A caveat is the level of challenge of self-selected books; readers who are engaged independently must be reading books they can handle. Sustained Silent Reading (SSR) time in school has yielded equivocal results, but engaged time at home and elsewhere is truly important. You, as teacher, need to model the fact that you are a reader and a collector of words. Share your writer's notebook with your students, particularly your collection of new and interesting words.

The National Reading Panel (NRP) recommendation that school time not be allotted for sustained reading is controversial. It was suggested that equivocal results were due to mis-implementation of SSR and that schools are doing their children a disservice if they fail to provide school time for engagement in the whole act of reading.

Advocate for Ongoing Staff Development

Teachers need training and continued support if they are to optimally help young adolescents to progress on the literacy continuum. Teachers (all teachers) need to learn about the strategies that are effective for expository text. Further, they need to be shown ways they can actively help their students in vocabulary knowledge and development. Teachers need some theoretical grounding, for it's not enough just to have the necessary tools in the proverbial carpenter's kit. You must also learn what tool to use and when. The traditional "stand and deliver" model of professional development has been found to be lacking. A job-embedded model that involves ongoing visitations, study groups, and reflection is much more likely to yield long-term improvement.

Content Reading and Writing Are Critical

It's a giant leap for many young adolescents from a self-contained elementary school classroom to a departmentalized middle grade school. The demands on teachers can be eased somewhat by good learning practices. Stereotypically, however, elementary-trained teachers see their role as teaching children, whereas their secondary-trained counterparts want to teach content. Content area teachers need to be aware that young adolescents need explicit strategic instruction in order to deal with expository texts that contain unfamiliar vocabulary and text structures.

Ensure Adult Role Models

RYAN

Ryan was a seventh grader in my class who was a "tough sell" when it came to book choices. He had turned up his nose at many of my suggestions, until a young assistant coach and rugby player recommended that he read The Time Machine *(Wells, 1988). Ryan loved the book, and then immersed himself in the genre and the author.*

Adults need to share their tastes in reading, for they never know when they'll strike a responsive chord. Adult "guest readers" can also have impact, as can buddy programs, where middle schoolers become models for younger children. It is particularly important to involve male models/guests because reading is often seen as a feminine activity.

REASONS FOR OPTIMISM

In upcoming chapters you will find a variety of rich, deep vocabulary learning strategies. All of them are rooted in the need for students to be active agents in their learning.

There is a silver lining in the news that despite the proliferation of less-than-enlightened practices, so many of our children still manage to learn so many words. If teachers would simply embrace the notion of "time-cost relationship" (upcoming), then it could "strengthen" word study greatly. We know that students are exposed to an incredible variety of words in classrooms where teachers provide many diverse and rich choices. Independent reading and the talk that bubbles up around students' reading and writing dramatically increases their word knowledge as well.

Aggregated standardized testing information can shed some light on your school or district's program. In these days of hyper-accountability, we must be aware of the tests' influences. And we can teach comprehension and vocabulary formats as another genre—if we don't, we're doing our students a disservice. Beyond the tests, a variety of language/literacy competencies can be demonstrated through portfolios, performances, and other artifacts. Students should be involved in self-assessment and have ownership, as in student-led conferences. More elusive to measure, but equally important, are teacher competence and administrative support.

Words can indeed be wonderful. And learning about words can be exciting and motivating for all students. A former colleague likened his vocabulary teaching to a "stevedore model": they'd metaphorically back the trucks up to the docks, and he'd fill 'em up! Next! Then it dawned on him that he was doing too much of the work, that students were "loaded" due to his hard work, but they were un-invested in the load. He gradually learned to build a word study system where he still worked hard, but he also worked smart—as did they. The results were solid enough to ensure that he'd never go back to teaching the way he had been taught.

This chapter has given a broad view of the unique characteristics of middle level children, as well as some overarching programmatic considerations. You've possibly started to make some word-learning connections, but if you're like most teachers, you are looking for specifics (they're coming!), for things you can do at 10:47 a.m. tomorrow. Here we go!

Chapter Two

What Works: Principles of Sound Vocabulary Instruction

To teach is to learn twice.

—Antoine Joubert

VOCABULARY SELECTION

I am in teacher Carey Little's fourth grade classroom now. Her students are abuzz with excitement. They have been "collecting" vocabulary from their Sustained Silent Reading books as well as their core novels, and each child has selected his or her top ten to present to the cooperative groups for trading, sorting, and, eventually, some games of Shazam! Each word is written in isolation on one side of a 5x8 card (see figure 2.1), with the student/owner/contributor also placing on the card both his or her initials and the source.

On the reverse side, the word is written in partial context, and a definition is given. The children go over their own words excitedly, going back to the texts as necessary, deciding on each group's top ten from among the forty to fifty total words. Some of those words go to the word wall, for public consumption. After more lively discussion, and some trading, the remaining cards are dumped into cans, and the groups start their Shazam! games.

Learning new words can be a great deal of fun. As this chapter unfolds, I will take the broad strokes and theoretical underpinnings I've outlined and narrow them to specific strategies. Depending on your students' needs and

Date	...the decrepit old house
	stood high on the hill...
decrepit (adj)	p.24
JG/ Blubber	broken down, weakened by old age

Figure 2.1.   Word Card (decrepit)

the context of the learning task, you can choose from a variety of strategies in your repertoire.

Everything the teacher does is predicated upon the need for active engagement of the students, as they connect known to the unknown. One broad consideration is identical for all word study: the teacher must foster active learning and exercise judgment based on her knowledge of her students and the situation (let's call this "Need/Context"). Then she makes the call.

As an example, imagine you are about to embark upon a social studies unit that will require students to understand well the word "propaganda." Based on your past teaching of the unit, coupled with your knowledge of this year's students' needs, you choose to *direct* the whole class using the Frayer Model. The Frayer Model (see chapter 5 for full treatment) requires lots of thoughtful teacher planning, and a good half hour of interaction between/among students. It takes a lot of time, which in the above context is necessary. You budget half an hour, "expensive" in terms of time, for the one word to be thoroughly and actively processed.

In another situation, you have five groups of five students involved in literature circles, each group reading a different title. Going through the same essential thought process similar to the propaganda example earlier, this time you opt to assign the Vocabulary Self-Selection Strategy (see chapter 4), with each child choosing fifteen to twenty words to be recorded and shared in a manner similar to the vignette in Carey Little's classroom. The students will be much more autonomous than in the earlier Frayer context, but there will still be much accountability.

Carol Tomlinson has created a general continuum of student independence (see figure 2.2) that can be applied specifically to vocabulary study. The astute teacher learns which students need less of her attention; she can then focus her efforts on directly moving her other students, *gradually*, toward independence in word learning. Once the teacher knows what her students'

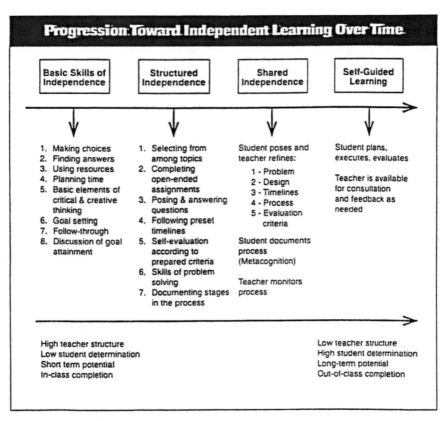

Figure 2.2. Tomlinson Continuum
Reprinted with Permission of NMSA. C. A. Tomlinson (1993). Independent study: A flexible tool for academic and personal growth. *Middle School Journal,* 25, 55–59.

capabilities are in terms of word work, she can then adjust the tasks according to context.

Teacher-directed (but still student-active) strategies and activities are at one end of the continuum; more student-controlled strategies and activities are at the other.

The teacher considers options along the continuum shown in figure 2.3, which is only a partial representation of the strategies at her disposal. She will consider many factors along the way! Sometimes she is directive and "telling" oriented; sometimes she's a manager and coach. "SFA" on the continuum is Semantic Feature Analysis (see chapter 5). It is a cousin to the Frayer Model in its intensity, but it results in deep knowledge of words.

Vocabulary instruction will vary based on what the learner already knows and the level of knowledge that is needed for understanding. There are many

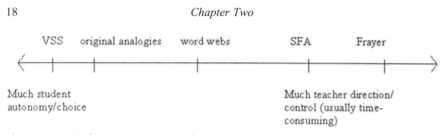

Figure 2.3.   Student Autonomy Continuum

ways to organize the vast (and sometimes conflicting) quantity of research that exists on effective vocabulary instruction. Some major factors to incorporate/consider are motivation, active involvement, choice, release of control, and efficient use of time. These are not mutually exclusive. For example, student motivation increases as a result of choice and active involvement.

It's recursive and messy and idiosyncratic. Furthermore, also entangled are teacher and student strategies that are fostered: teachers model "talking off the tops of their heads" (Allen, 1999) and thinking aloud in order to make the implicit, explicit—but the corollary is that for deep understanding and long-term retention, students need to do the same things. That being said, here are my guidelines for effective vocabulary instruction.

GRADUALLY RELINQUISH RESPONSIBILITY

All good learners take control of their learning. For the teacher, the goal of vocabulary instruction is to often be a facilitator, a guide on the side. What's tricky is that in order to be an effective guide on the side, you've first got to be, ironically, an expert other, a model, the sage on the stage.

Pearson and Gallagher (1983) developed the classic model for gradual release of responsibility for comprehension instruction, which transfers nicely for word work. In this model, the teacher moves from total responsibility, gradually, to a situation where students have internalized the strategy and can apply it independently. The art of vocabulary teaching rests in the ability to know how much scaffolding to provide and when to remove it—this gets into the assessment realm, to follow in chapter 10.

Students need, for example, thoughtful instruction to learn how to use the dictionary and the thesaurus, as well as the glossary. Using these tools can be complex and difficult. Some students, when admonished to "look it up," cannot find the word, let alone ascertain which of the multiple meanings is appropriate. We all can recount stories from the tragic to the sublime, such as the child who noted that "erodes" means "eats out" and produced the sentence

"Since my mom went back to work, my family erodes a lot." Students need explicit, meaningful instruction and follow-up practice in order to find the "just right" word for written or oral communications.

Students are perfectly capable of discerning what they need to know—and those results are much longer lasting (that is, learning "sticks"). The work of Ruddell and Shearer (2002) suggests that control through self-selection is an important factor in building a generalized vocabulary. Other researchers examined both the challenge level as well as retention of student-selected words—students consistently chose words at or above grade level for study. It may also be wise to do collaborative word selection, particularly for content area learning, with the teacher balancing student choices with selections of her own—again, control can and should be gradually relinquished to students.

Similarly, instruction on using context clues as well as structural analysis should move gradually from teacher directed to student controlled. Again, it is preferable for such instruction to be embedded in authentic literature. Dictionary use alone often results in sentences such as "Dad came home with a cliché (worn out expression) on his face" whereas overlapping context clues coupled with tangible examples and necessary explanation will better serve children. Teachers should never forget the power of the anecdote, either. Quick little stories or illustrations often tip the scales in favor of retention of meaning.

BUILD A WORD-RICH ENVIRONMENT

Middle school students need "word-aware" classrooms, visually as well as symbolically, that invite both incidental learning and explicit instruction. Students and teachers are aware that word knowledge is both caught and taught.

Younger students are often flooded with environmental print; the counterpart for older students is the graffiti board. The graffiti board can simply be a wall covered with butcher paper, where students are invited to "share." With teacher contributions and modeling, a temporary and decorative form of word wall is created, with students contributing words, slogans, lyrics of favorite songs, and pictures. Puzzles, word games, and, yes, even dictionaries, abound in a word-aware room. This type of learning sends powerful messages—although exposure alone cannot fully generate the learning of specific vocabulary words, it can help to develop a wide, usable general vocabulary in a classroom culture steeped in words, words, and more words!

Wide reading of a variety of genres by and to young people coupled with attention to words is, of course, a must. In short, word learning permeates everything that teachers do each day, rather than formal, traditional "vocabulary instruction." Students should become attuned to listening for new and interesting words, and this disposition should be celebrated and practiced constantly. Teachers are, of course, models of word learning; they should show a genuine interest in word learning, recount anecdotes, and generally model vocabulary enthusiasm and curiosity.

TEACHERS THINK ALOUD
(AND TEACH STUDENTS TO DO THE SAME)

Originally attributed to Davey (1983), thinking aloud can be used by teachers or students. Additionally, when used with students, it can be done with groups or with individuals. Thinking aloud is a powerful way to make the invisible, visible.

When students think aloud, they verbalize their thoughts and reveal the strategies they are using. Their thoughts at the word level might include predicting, fix-up strategies, or even confusion. These "windows" to see inside the child's head are useful to the teacher as well as to the reader/learner, for in the latter case it certainly aids monitoring and metacognitive processes. Thinking aloud puts the responsibility on learners to become aware of how (and whether) they derive meaning.

Students need to observe teacher modeling and then have varied opportunities for practice: whole class, in pairs, and individually. A bridge to thinking aloud can be as simple as having students write down questions and comments as they read. Post-it notes are useful for this.

TEACHERS PROVIDE TIME FOR READING

Student engagement in the integrated act of reading is still the most significant determiner of vocabulary growth. It's complex and fraught with difficulties. But teachers must see to it that students "do it" (the whole act) often. There is a school of thought that holds that "[r]ather than allocating instructional time for independent reading in the classroom, encourage your students to read more outside of school" (National Reading Panel, 2000, p. 29). That sentence dismisses the power of SSR (Sustained Silent Reading) and ignores the reality of the home lives of many of our children. Yes, many children do lots of wide reading outside of school—but it all starts with the motivational and valuing messages of setting aside "company time" for *just reading* in school—on school time!

TEACHERS CREATE MOTIVATION
FOR VOCABULARY LEARNING

Building and maintaining student motivation for vocabulary learning is a major challenge. Academic motivation in general is a fragile commodity and, for many students, it declines as they progress in school (McKenna & Kear, 1990; National Endowment for the Arts, 2007; Unrau & Schlackman, 2006). Although children come to their early schooling experiences expecting to do well, something goes wrong along the way for many of them. For academic motivation to remain high, students must perceive that they are successful. Accordingly, teachers who are effective recognize the power of interest and choice.

TEACHERS USE ASSESSMENTS EFFECTIVELY

Assessment is simply gathering information for specific purposes. Summative assessment (typically in norm-referenced tests) is a reality in today's high-stakes environment. Blachowicz and Fisher (2010) state that it is helpful to think of two main dimensions for vocabulary knowledge: depth and breadth. Depth refers to how much is known about a particular word, whereas breadth is concerned primarily with how a word is connected to others in a domain of learning. These constructs relate to assessment because many of the instructional techniques that follow can also be used as assessment tools.

TEACHERS MODEL GOOD WORD-LEARNING BEHAVIORS

Good teaching recognizes that successful learners are active agents who construct their knowledge. Of course, discussions are a simple but effective way to involve young people in examining the nuances of words. Additionally, learning clusters of words during meaningful teachable moments (for example, ace, stroke, serve, and baseline have specific meanings in a tennis context) makes sense to middle school students, especially.

Thoughtful questioning techniques require students to discern different features of word meaning. It is critical that students answer and explain their reasoning for answers to questions such as "Would a sedentary person enjoy an aerobics class?" or "Would an intellectual have a limited vocabulary?"

Personalizing learning is another strategy of effective teachers and learners. Words not learned in firsthand experience can also be personalized by relating the new to the already known. Creating one's own mnemonic or image is an example of a way to personalize meaning. Keyword methods are the best known of these learning strategies. Students are taught to create a verbal connection, an image, or a picture to help cement the meaning in memory. Verbal labels are then coupled with pictures and memory for the word. For example, Roger was struggling with the word "epitaph" versus "epithet." He chose to consult *The People's Almanac* (Wallechensky & Wallace, 1975), and he collected some amusing epitaphs to share on the graffiti board.

Another sound practice involves active involvement of students in constructing word meaning through the use of semantic webs, organizers, maps, or other relational charts. Many studies have shown the efficacy of putting word meaning into graphic form. It is prudent to remember, however, that mere *construction* of such maps, without *discussion*, is not in and of itself effective. Without talk, sharing, and application of the word, the map is not optimally effective.

For learning specific words, providing students with multiple sources of information, coupled with opportunities to use the words in meaningful communication situations, results in superior word learning. Teaching definitions results in some learning. However, definitional approaches that overlap with active processing are far superior. In effective vocabulary-learning classrooms, students encounter words in context but are also provided with additional opportunities to learn appropriate definitions, synonyms, and analogies.

Following are some further reminders about vocabulary instruction:

Wide reading must be planned, enticing, rewarded, and rewarding. So, too, must be direct instruction. Every lesson, every day presents teachable moments to be capitalized upon. Teachers who know the implications of the research are deliberate about increasing the number of "exposures" to new words their students encounter, which connects nicely to another important tenet.

Reading or hearing a new word is a good thing, and (eventually) if it's heard "enough" times in "enough" contexts, it will be absorbed. But why wait for these exposures to occur naturally? With techniques such as "text talks," teachers can be very purposeful about contexts and definitions (and anecdotes) to deliberately create efficiency to speed up word-learning probabilities. It's akin to the creation of pearls. Pearls do occur naturally. But they can also be propagated. Text talks are examples of "anchored" vocabulary instruction: the teacher helps the children to pull out the targeted word, manipulate it, then put it back where it belongs—in a meaningful context.

Yes, we want to stretch our students. However, we want the stretch to be worth it, so that they learn "rich" words they'll encounter again. The teacher needs to decide what words merit allocation of instructional time! A discussion of a four-level framework, for example, is found in Flanigan and

Greenwood (2007). These authors adapted the model of Beck, McKeown, and Kucan (2002) in terms of selecting which words to teach. Sometimes we need to pretty much *tell* students in the beginning, but our goals should be to teach so that they can apply the words in different situations, involving them in active construction of meaning. Webbing, for example, should not be done randomly or carelessly—the teacher must be systematic in organizing information.

You probably remember being assigned the onerous task of having to use ten or fifteen rather obtuse new words in an "original" story; "It was a *dark, stormy* night" might become "It was an *ebony, tempestuous* night." No, we're talking about having kids generate, more selectively, more meaningfully. When using words in sentences, students do need to be taught to elaborate, to provide an enriched context that demonstrates deep understanding.

You as teacher need to do a particularly good job of "telling" in these cases, and it's a good time to be up front about the inexactness/imprecision of context clues. Be very direct if the context is insufficient to ascertain a word's meaning.

In addition to such instruction, students need the "permission" and the safety of a low-risk environment, in order to try on words for fit and to play with language. Students will only gain control of new words by using them, and this requires the teacher to recognize (and communicate!) that mistakes are not pathological! When students use words in conversation, in writing, and in word play, a deeper understanding of vocabulary develops. Words are then gradually known well and are used flexibly and willingly.

TEACHERS ANALYZE TIME-COST TRADEOFF

Seemingly contradictory conclusions can be drawn from the failure of some traditional vocabulary instruction to improve reading comprehension. Since comprehension of texts requires knowledge much richer than simply learning the definitions of words, in some cases vocabulary instruction must be rich enough to really teach students new concepts. The extreme responses, at either end of the continuum, would be (a) to devote the bulk of the school day to intensive vocabulary instruction or (b) to abandon vocabulary instruction altogether.

Although wide reading is the major avenue of acquiring in-depth knowledge of words, there clearly is a place for middle ground. The resolution lies in the teacher's ability to make *efficient* use of vocabulary instruction. She must assess the text, her own purposes, and her students, and identify the words and concepts that are likely to pose serious difficulties for students.

Since naturally occurring context is faulty (as previously laid out) and comprehension of (particularly content area) texts may crucially depend on knowledge of specific words, the teacher must find the proper balance between incidental learning and explicit instruction.

Intensive instruction is warranted to produce word knowledge of any depth. It also requires time to plan and to execute. Only a small fraction of potentially unknown words merit the intensive time required by, for example, the aforementioned Frayer Model. In general, most story/narrative readings do not require intensive vocabulary instruction. It would be a mis-expenditure of time to build a model, or a mobile, or a diorama of a word.

To comprehend narrative text, the reader can be fuzzy on the meaning of a few words per page. But in the content areas, intensive vocabulary instruction is particularly useful when new and difficult concepts are under study. Nagy (1988) called this ability to evaluate the tradeoff; that is, when to allocate the necessary instructional time for direct instruction vis-à-vis immersion, the *time-cost relationship*. Intensive instruction is relatively expensive, and only a fraction of the words that students must learn can be "covered."

If the teacher uses good judgment about what and how to teach, children will benefit. "Only if one feels free from the obligation to teach about every unfamiliar word in a selection is there any time to treat any of the words in depth" (Nagy, 1988, p. 39). We as teachers cannot do it all, but we can do some of "it" efficiently, strategically, wisely, and economically. Effective teachers must devote planned instruction to the introduction of new words. Additionally, follow-up is crucial, as you shall see.

Beck and McKeown (2003) developed a model for the teaching of "sophisticated words," that is, new concepts or new labels for previously known concepts. Their procedure involved text talks, a read-aloud approach. They researched instruction of the targeted words *during* and *after* reading.

- *During* reading, to forestall comprehension difficulties, the word was simply told, for example, "forlorn means very, very sad."
- *After* reading, direct and lively instruction was used. The words were contextualized; that is, they were situated in the story. The teachers would then move beyond the story context. For example, "Forlorn means very, very sad. Say the word with me: forlorn. Would you be forlorn on your birthday? Forlorn means more than just a little bit sad, it means very, very sad."
- Beck and McKeown found that just reading aloud, without any explanation, resulted in a 4 to 15 percent chance of the word being learned. With rich explanation, however, the chance of word learning rose from 15 to 40 percent. The results were clearly educationally significant. The more instruction the students received, the better they did in terms of word learning and retention. Rich instruction was good; *richer* instruction was better.

- Yet teachers still must go back to the basic *time-cost* principle mentioned earlier. There are plenty of good word-learning strategies for all teachers to incorporate and pass on to their students—text talks are *good*, for they involve sound underpinnings—but teachers need to be mindful of how much time these (and any other) procedures "cost," balanced with the benefits for children. It's a fine line for teachers to walk. It's important, for example, for a fourth grader to know the word "musher" before reading a passage about the Iditarod. But when will he need that word again?

Many children's best chance to learn rich language often comes from school talk, assigned reading, and being read to. Virtually all children recognize and are facile with the "high frequency" top words, but it's the number of "rarer" words in the children's (and adults') total word bank that distinguishes the strong from the weaker: readers, writers, *and* speakers.

So text talking is a good, research-based strategy. At the same time, you as instructional decision maker must remember to resist the temptation to teach too many words; rather, you must orchestrate the disposition and inclination for children to take over eventual control of word learning as much as is developmentally appropriate.

Learning of new words is not a simple issue. Though there is much still to be learned about vocabulary acquisition, we do know enough about it to not fall back into the ineffective practices of the past. We know better and our children deserve better.

SPECIAL NEEDS: ENGLISH LANGUAGE LEARNERS

We want all students to develop rich receptive and expressive vocabularies, so they may read, write, understand, and speak effectively. An extensive vocabulary, particularly in light of its relationship to reading comprehension, is surely a ticket to enfranchisement and probable success in schooling.

Most of the principles and underpinnings outlined earlier (relinquishing control to students, connecting the new to the known) apply to students with special needs as well as other students. Each and every child is special in some sense, and special needs vocabulary learners range from the gifted to those needy youngsters who bear an alphabet soup of labels: SED (Socially and Emotionally Disturbed), PDD (Pervasive Developmental Disorder), LD (Learning Disabled). Then there are the unfortunate children who have had little exposure to books and language. This section, however, will focus on English language learners (ELLs).

Speakers of English only, somewhat ironically, are often taken aback when they learn that people who speak only one language form a minority of the world's population. Simply put, the majority of the world's population is bilingual (or more). That being the case, it is puzzling why so much attention is devoted by the English-speaking world to the matter of learning an additional language.

Given *time* and *opportunity*, most people can learn as many languages as necessary. In school, teachers must judiciously allocate those two precious commodities. Yet there is a critical understanding that complicates the proposition: children who come to school with some degree of proficiency in more than one language are usually immigrants or the children of immigrants. Some function quite nicely in both languages, but some are limited, particularly in vocabulary.

These children might be reasonably considered to be bilingual, but they need to, in fact, become trilingual: they need to learn a third language, namely, Standard English, the language of schooling. Children learn a second language at home rather naturally, but school language is trickier. "Children move from the concrete, meaning-centered language of the home to the abstract, inward focused and largely decontextualized language of the school. As one child put it, 'teachers seem to talk about things that aren't there!'" (Piper, 1993, p. 15).

Vocabulary presents a special challenge for children in ESL or bilingual classes. And teachers need to recognize that fluency in social English can mask real difficulty in dealing with mainstream content area vocabulary and comprehension. Following are some broad understandings, gleaned from the literature.

Wide Reading

The research is quite clear about the relationship among reading engagement, vocabulary, and comprehension—with doses of motivation added to the mix. Wide reading needs to be done in enjoyable and relatively easy material, by all children.

The stakes are higher for your ELL children, and it is imperative that you get them reading the right books. Be sure to get some reading material specifically for your ELLs. Graves, Juel, and Graves (2004) suggest that teachers collect short and simple selections containing fairly easy vocabulary, selections containing more challenging vocabulary, and selections in students' native language. "Also, if available, materials that include both a version in students' native language and an English version are very valuable" (p. 239).

Other Instructional Suggestions

Following are some other recommendations that should be of use in maximizing ELLs vocabulary learning in school.

Capitalize on the "borrowed" nature of English.

The eclectic origins of English are very well-known. This has left us with a massive number of words to know; the good news is that English is similar to so many languages (for example, à la carte, dormitory, vaudeville, quiche, and bureau from French). Help your ELLs to recognize the contributions of their native language.

Help children with idioms and connotations.

English words are combined in a variety of ways, and these combinations (even compounds) are notorious for not equating neatly to their component parts. The compound "doghouse" makes sense to a second language learner; the expression "in the doghouse" may not. "Bombshell," as another example, has literal and figurative meaning. Teachers must actively teach children to use context clues; when context doesn't suffice, children may need to memorize the expression and its meaning.

Remember that immersion alone is insufficient for school learning.

Just as students catch a cold or the flu, they can naturally pick up some vocabulary. It most likely will not be the vocabulary necessary to succeed in school, however. Although ELLs do need exposure to academic language, they need systematic, explicit instruction in English language systems. Harper and deJong (2004) recommended that Reciprocal Teaching (Palinscar & Brown, 1984) be modified. In the adaptation, language cue cards are provided and strategy roles are practiced in order to provide the necessary linguistic scaffolding.

Be steadfastly child centered.

Honor, and build upon, each child's previous experience, language, and culture.

Literature-Based instruction is good.

And authentic. And motivating. Mohr (2004) reminds us that reading experiences provide "comprehensible input" that is necessary for development of academic vocabulary. Big books and picture books should be read aloud. Mohr also recommends repeated readings of several different or bilingual versions in order to reinforce vocabulary. She advocates careful text reflection, followed by use of the books to generate discussion and writing. These strategies, of course, are good for non-ELL students as well.

Judiciously emulate the language learning of home.

Any vocabulary learner, even a highly motivated individual, can progress only so far under artificial or contrived circumstances.

Remember the power of student talk.

Staab (1991) found that teacher talk plus quiet time accounted for 78 percent of the time in third and sixth grade classrooms. In, say, a five-hour day, little time is meted out to students. Remember, "teaching isn't talking and learning isn't listening; it's just the opposite." According to Mohr (2004), teachers must be persistent in planning for group work and expecting that ELLs be more than passive spectators. She recommends that teachers come back to these students and delve deeply in order to elaborate or extend their responses. Mohr contends that teachers need to ask more questions, even if it entails giving students choices for their response.

Enlist the aid of parents.

Caregivers have a powerful role in preparing their children for school through language and literacy activities in the home. Walberg (1984) contends that parent involvement and home factors are more important for student achievement than a variety of other factors: educational strategies, increased academic learning time, and environmental factors, to name a few.

It is critical that parents of ELLs be purposefully enfranchised. Parents can enrich teachers' understanding of their students' attitudes toward and preferences for literacy learning. Well-planned workshops and demonstrations can teach parents how to read with their children, how to question in order to promote higher order thinking skills, and how to help make the reading-writing connection.

Have high expectations for all learners.

Harper and de Jong (2004) make the point that ELLs do differ significantly from other diverse learners, and that instructors should not simply equate the process of learning a first language with that of learning a second language. Mohr (2004) states that teachers who expect a lot from their students must also be prepared to provide the necessary scaffolding/support. Mohr states, as well, that in addition to language "skills," ELLs need to have work in more general understandings and expectations that will ensure success.

Use thematic units to enhance vocabulary.

"Thematic instruction makes sense for all students for many reasons, but ELLs certainly benefit from dwelling on a topic long enough to build and extend conceptual and linguistic knowledge" (Mohr, 2004, p. 22). Targeted vocabulary can be applied, reinforced, and strengthened as opposed to being merely introduced. Mohr goes on to remind us that integrated approaches and social interaction result in vocabulary growth.

In conclusion, the need for ELL students to develop rich and flexible vocabularies is unquestioned. Yet the task of teaching, facilitating, and promoting such word work is complex, messy, and fraught with difficulty. What's been presented here should aid and abet you in tackling this enormous, very important, and necessary task.

In the way of overall summation of this chapter, the groundwork has been laid for the bulk of this book. Principles and underpinnings have been laid out, and specific activities and strategies will now be woven into what is to come. You have had some of the why, and soon it will be time for the how.

Chapter Three

What's to Come: Indirect, Direct, General, and Specific Methodologies

I'm not a very good writer, but I'm an excellent rewriter.

—James Michener

In chapters 1 and 2 we introduced some broad whys of this book: topic, purpose, and principles. If you are a practitioner, you could quite possibly be having a classic "yeah but" moment, as in "yeah, but when is he going to give us specifics that we can use at 10:47 a.m. tomorrow?"

This is intended to be a brief transitional chapter in which I cover less theory and begin to deal with the practicalities and nuances of vocabulary instruction. In this chapter you will see the overall graphic organizer, and you will garner some information on some very important indirect and general strategies, structures, and methodologies: structural analysis and word parts, dictionaries and other "tools" of reference, context clues, wide self-selected reading, and oral language and listening. These are powerful and important considerations that need to be addressed before really delving into the remainder of this book.

THE ORGANIZER

Early feedback from peers indicated that my drafts of graphic organizers did not get the job done well. As the content grew, so did the organizer. Soon it got unmanageable.

In the second draft, the organizer was broken apart, but continuity was lost. *Now* we have something workable.

Figure 3.1 gives a visual representation of vocabulary learning based on information presented in *Put Reading First* (Armbruster, Lehr, & Osborn, 2001), a guide designed by teachers for teachers that describes the findings of the National Reading Panel (NRP) report (2000). The authors make the distinction between broad "opportunities" as opposed to the intentional and direct instruction methodologies for word learning; these are further split into specific word-instruction methods and more generic word-learning strategies. In my rendition of the NRP's work, the *specific strategies* (for narrative, content area, and writing instruction) will be covered in the chapters 4, 5, and 6. The *general word-learning strategies* (e.g., context clues, structural analysis, dictionary skills) are very transportable and interplay with other word learning.

We will "break out" this overall organizer, presenting various sections of it in specific chapters. This will allow us to zoom in on some of the strategies quite specifically. At the same time, we'll be able to consider how the parts fit together.

Figure 3.1 will serve as the overall organizer. For each chapter, it tells us where we'll find details that aid us in making sense of the big picture.

Several chapters, however, will have "blown-out" organizers that delineate more details. Most important will be figures 4.1, 5.1, and 6.1, which will address the specific word-learning strategies for narrative text, the content areas, and writing. These fit with the overall organization, but provide more specifics and help to make it all more meaningful.

A word of caution concerning the separation/categorization of the strategies into the aforementioned categories: go with the best fit. The Frayer Model, for example, is absolutely best suited for content area teaching. Likewise, Vocabulary Self-Selection (VSS) belongs and fits well for narrative text. Many of the other specific word-learning strategies do not fit so tidily into one of the three designated areas (that is, vocabulary for narrative or informational or writing purposes). They are separated artificially but purposefully, but the lines that segregate them are blurred.

VOCABULARY AND ORAL LANGUAGE

As you glance at figure 3.1, please note the box labeled "Indirect Instruction." The word is used loosely, for by the time students reach the ages/grades that are within the purview of this book, most of the rich will have gotten richer, and, unfortunately, the poor will have gotten poorer, as I will explain.

Students from homes rich in conversation have heard more than 45 million words by the time they are four. On the other hand, children from less

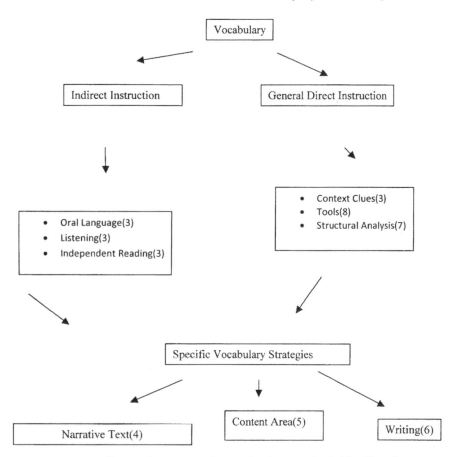

Figure 3.1. Overall Organizer. Note: The number in parenthesis identifies chapter.
Created by Scott C. Greenwood based on narrative information from *Put Reading First* (2001).

advantaged homes have heard as few as 13 million words. Research has documented the huge head start enjoyed by most middle class children, in terms of both productive and receptive language.

Research on adult conversation indicates a basic vocabulary of about five thousand words, with an additional five thousand used less frequently. According to Trelease (1995), beyond the ten thousand word benchmark are the "rare" words—the words that play a critical role in reading. The number of rare words we understand and can use determines the power of our vocabularies.

The spontaneous processes of learning to listen and speak are closely connected to the educational process of learning to read and write. Proponents of whole language contend that reading and writing are natural acts and that meaningful immersion is sufficient for most children to become literate. But reading and writing are "less natural" than listening and speaking, and Tom Gill, a former colleague, reminded his students that bears can be taught to ride bicycles. A few (very few!) children learn to read on their own, by immersion. Oral language development is certainly a big factor in vocabulary development, which connects to comprehension, which connects to educational success, which often is related to success in life.

"Knowing" a word involves moving through a range of meanings and forms. Words are not either known or unknown: as with most new learning, new vocabulary words and concepts are learned by degree. Additionally, what constitutes a word depends on who is counting: think of all the words that have many meanings and many forms. For example, "brig" (as you will soon see) can be part of the tally four times, once for each definition, then twice more for the plural of each.

Understanding what one hears or reads precedes learning to produce the word orally or in writing. The productive vocabulary (speaking and writing) is never as large as the comprehension vocabulary (listening and reading) for either children or adults.

Word learning continues throughout life. And since the English lexicon contains over 2 million words, there is no need to worry about running out—even if we continued learning three thousand words every year, we would have to live to be over six hundred years old before we learned the whole 2 million. As we move on to listening, the flip side of speaking, remember that they complement each other—and start to think of what you might do to help those of your students who have impoverished listening and speaking backgrounds.

LISTENING

Another part of Indirect Instruction in Figure 3.1 is listening, an act that students often are expected to spend inordinate amounts of time on in school. Teachers often assume that intermediate grade (and older) students come to them able to listen and speak competently—they may notice, however, that their students don't always choose to listen and speak well. This may be due to practice in "schooling" where the daily routine includes heavy doses of TTSL (teacher talk, student listen).

Remember, vocabulary proficiency grows from listening competence to oral competence to written competence. The words and concepts students absorb and use as they listen and talk are the foundation for what they read and write.

If children are sitting quietly in rows while the teacher talks, they *may* be listening. If they are doing some sort of seat work, they may be engaged and interested (but usually not, for they probably do not have any choice, and the challenge level may or may not be appropriate). At times, the teacher needs to maximize student talking and student listening.

Obviously, the best structure would be pairs, then triads, then groups of four. The conversations don't have to be lengthy. You will need to demonstrate/model/scaffold for your students early in the year—a simple fishbowl technique works well. The teacher typically is one of the "fish" with a student partner (or two, or three). She takes the opportunity to think aloud and have the others do the same.

Vocabulary subgroups, whatever their size, must be taught the requisite social skills. As students read more, listen actively, and talk for authentic purposes, they grow in confidence and competence.

WIDE READING

Finally, figure 3.1 lists independent/self-selected reading under the "indirect" category. When the scientifically/research-based faction gained political control, they noted that the research on independent reading was equivocal. This, in turn, led to the mandate that students should read at home, that valuable instructional school time should not be "wasted" on a practice that was not evidence based. We know that wide reading is a powerful determiner of vocabulary growth. Wide readers have richer, deeper, and more extensive command of words.

Sustained silent reading (SSR) is the process of including independent reading in each day's instructional program. SSR can be tweaked in a variety of ways to maximize benefits for all students, but the bottom line is this: you cannot create a word aware classroom without wide reading. If the teacher is a reader, and he expects his students to read, they will read. It's all about messages, overt and covert. An astute teacher builds in class time for students to read books they have chosen, both at home and in school. Students are provided plenty of opportunities to share what they are reading, including vocabulary.

CONTEXT CLUES

Context clues are classified under "General Direct Instruction." You might choose to add adjectives such as "crucial" and "highly important"! Context clues have traditionally been misused, for they are often invoked but are rarely explicitly taught. It's akin to, at the decoding level, telling the children to "sound it out." They *would* sound it out if they could sound it out. Similarly, it's not particularly useful advice to tell children to "use context clues to figure it out"—they need to be shown how to do so, and teachers need to recognize the complexity of using the context. Consider the following passage:

> I was a sailor on a Spanish *brig* on its way from Veracruz in Mexico to Cadoz in April. We were sailing with a large cargo of silver. (Gaarder, 1996, p. 27)

A skilled reader who had never seen or heard the word "brig" before could readily make the inference necessary to decide that a brig was a type of ship. Few other inferences are required, but a single exposure does not result in a very rich or lasting understanding of the word. One student thought that the brig was a part of a ship, below the deck, where the captain stuck crew members for punishment. When he checked the dictionary, yes, the word was listed twice: "A two-masted sailing ship, square-rigged on both masts [short for brigantine]"; also "A ship's prison." In the case of brig, for me, some previous familiarity, plus context, plus the dictionary, plus a semi-authentic purpose resulted in richer understanding.

Now let's consider another passage from the same novel:

> Being hereditarily tainted, I sometimes tried to take part in Dad's philosophical discussions, which arose just about every time he wasn't talking about Mommy. (Gaarder, 1996, p. 19)

Let's assume that you tell a typical eighth grader to figure out the meaning of two unknowns, "hereditarily" and "tainted," by using the context and relating it to his or her background of experience. It's often just too much! Students need to be reading books of appropriate challenge, and they need to be taught to read on the lines, between the lines, and beyond the lines.

There is no question that learning from context is an important avenue of vocabulary growth and that it deserves attention and practice in the classroom. Just consider the fact that a student learns approximately 3,000 new words a year. Of the 3,000 only about 300 are learned by direct instruction, which leaves an impressive 2,700 that, by default, are largely learned naturally, via context and wide reading. But context, used as an instructional method by itself, is ineffective and very inefficient as a means of teaching new meanings, at least when compared with other forms of vocabulary instruction.

The problem is that, in many cases, context may look quite helpful if one already knows what a word means, but it seldom supplies adequate information for a person who has no other knowledge about the meaning of the word.

Consider the following sentence used to illustrate context clues involving contrast: "Although Melissa was very comely, her roommate was grotesque." The signal word "although" makes is clear that contrast is involved, but the exact nature of the contrast is clear only to someone who knows both comely and grotesque.

The problem becomes obvious when one attempts to substitute other words into the sentence—almost any contrasting pair would work: tall, short; smart, stupid; loud, quiet. And note that the preceding example involves the use of contrast, a relatively informative type of context clue!

The astute teacher must face this dilemma: most contexts in naturally occurring text are relatively uninformative. The context around any unfamiliar word tells us something about its meaning, but seldom does any single context give complete information. Both experience and research provide ample support for teaching students how to use context. Students who read grade-level texts under natural conditions have about a 5 to 20 percent chance of learning meaning from a single exposure. Further, if average fifth graders spend about twenty-five minutes a day reading, they encounter about twenty thousand unfamiliar words.

If the aforementioned 5 percent (or one twentieth) of those words can be figured out from context, a child, while reading, would learn about a thousand new words from that strategy. It's common sense that that amount of time reading is the best predictor of vocabulary growth. Your author is certainly not advocating abandonment of the use of context—rather, instructional strategies will be presented so that instructors can expand their active teaching of the use of context clues and increase the amount of time that students spend reading. An example of this is found in an article by Greenwood and Flanigan (2007) that provides specifics on overlapping context clues and semantic gradients.

Please remember, as you read on, that the methodologies are rarely used in isolation in the real world. They need to be internalized by teachers and students alike, then applied fluidly, flexibly, and appropriately.

To summarize what is known from the research about context clues, Baumann and Kameenui (1991) make the following three points:

1. Context clues are relatively ineffective means for inferring the meaning of specific words. McKeown and Beck (1991) explain the varying reliability of context clues by developing four classifications: directive contexts, general contexts, non-directive contexts, and misdirective contexts (p. 22–23).
2. Students are more apt to learn specific new vocabulary when definitional information is combined with contextual clues, as opposed to when contextual analysis is used in isolation.

3. Research on teaching contextual analogies as transferable and generalizable strategies for word learning is promising but limited.

You just had the quick version of the context clues tutorial. Additionally, you've beefed up your knowledge of the connectivity among speaking, listening, writing, and wide reading. The first three chapters have been mostly about general (i.e., transportable) methodologies that enable incidental learning. Done well, they still require expert teaching. *Now* we'll delve into specifics!

Chapter Four

Vocabulary and Narrative Text

The great thing about collecting words is that they're free; you can borrow them, trade them in, or toss them out. Words are lightweight, portable, and they're everywhere.

—Susan G. Woolridge, in "Poemcrazy"

JEFF: CONTEXT

*Jeff Singleton is working his fifth grade language arts class through a survival unit: he has four groups of six children each reading one of four titles—*Hatchet *(Paulson, 1996),* Sign of the Beaver *(Speare, 1983),* Dear Mr. Henshaw *(Cleary, 1984), and* Julie of the Wolves *(George, 1973). I stop into his room while he has the* Julie of the Wolves *group involved in thinking aloud for the purpose of some vocabulary learning. Jeff does a masterful job of modeling how he uses overlapping information to figure out new words by using context clues:*

Gang, reading is thinking, it's that simple. You gotta know when you don't know, first of all. "Julie trudged *across the frozen tundra." Let's see . . . hmmm. If I was a typical fifth grader and didn't know "trudged" in isolation, I'd sure have a good shot at its meaning in the sentence. Who knows? Yeah, Jake? (Jake says "walked.")*

Now, here's what I'd be thinkin' . . . if the author wanted me to make a picture in my head—which good authors do—and she meant Julie walked, she would have used the word "walked." So I'm wondering why she used the word "trudged"—it's gotta either mean something different than walked, or it's gotta be a specific way of walking. So I'm

39

gonna go back to the passage and read beyond—both ways—where
trudged appeared.

Vocabulary instruction and comprehension instruction are intertwined, but for teaching, modeling, and demonstration they have been separated, for presentation purposes. Reading informational texts (i.e., content area) cannot be separated so tidily, either. Just like *Midnight in the Garden of Good and Evil* (Berendt, 1994) and *In Cold Blood* (Capote, 1965) crossed boundaries as "nonfiction novels," Miss Frizzle, of the Magic Schoolbus series, gets out of the box. We used to say that children read for pleasure or for information; now we know that informational texts can be very pleasurable.

That being said, parents rarely catch children reading their assigned social studies textbook under the covers, using a flashlight, after lights out. We shall go ahead and devote this chapter to strategies for children to take control of when they read "literature"—either as a whole class, reading a single title; flexibly grouped for guided reading; or independently.

A couple of other things need to be said up front. Children do plenty of reading in other genres, but for now we will stick with literature. Additionally, earlier we talked about gradually relinquishing control to students. Content area/technical strategies need more teacher scaffolding than those required for narrative text. Most agree that the narrative text demands are "lighter" than those of informational reading. That is, a fairly solid reader can adequately reach her goal for much of her narrative reading with three, four, possibly five unknown words per page. However, for informational reading—particularly that which is contingent on prior knowledge and motivation—specific strategies, often teacher controlled, need to be used in order to reduce the amount of unknowns. To do this costs time. Whereas students typically are expected to zip through thousands of pages of narrative text in a school year, the sheer volume of informational text is considerably less.

LITERATURE-BASED INSTRUCTION

Even in school districts that have adopted basal series (they tend to call them "programs" nowadays), authentic literature is often used for instruction at least part of the time. And some systems use authentic literature exclusively or primarily for reading instruction. The use of literature-based, "balanced" approaches has meant that teachers are confronted with teaching vocabulary (or having students try to learn vocabulary!) without the guidance of "teacher-proof" teacher's manuals: the publishers select the words to teach, define the words, and tell the teacher how to do it. For example, "Now point to the word 'aardvark.' Now ask if anyone knows what an aardvark is [answer is supplied just in case]."

In systems that don't use a basal, literature can be "basalized" by the lock-step use of commercially produced "packets" created to "help" the teacher. This often results in over-teaching of vocabulary and too much time on the novel. David Cooper, an eminent speaker and senior author for Houghton-Mifflin, referring to overkill of *Charlotte's Web* (White, 1952), once said, "You'd hate that little pig, too, after six weeks!"

The first problem is that rarely should all students be reading the same core novel, for the readability of a single title is typically "right" for only about one third of any class. The second problem is that teachers have to get over the notion that *they* must be the sole arbiter and purveyor of information in *selecting* and *teaching* vocabulary.

Successful utilization of literature in the middle grades requires a thoughtful balance of activities. Reading should be done *by* and *to* the students. In a balanced approach, shared reading, guided reading, and self-selected reading should take place daily, that is, reading aloud *to* children (this can be above their grade level, for the teacher is in control and can mediate—students are exposed to rich vocabulary and sophisticated content and syntax); reading *by* the students at their instructional level, with some teacher guidance; and reading *by* the students, *independently*, in and out of school, in "just right" books.

A key factor in successful implementation is, of course, having well-trained, confident, creative teachers. Additionally, access to a large number of books, consistent standards, and administrative support are essential. Personal conferences and differentiation of instruction (while, oxymoronically, teaching to the same standards using the same curriculum) are also necessary. In these classrooms students engage in grand conversations about what they've read, and they balance their own selections with teacher selections when it comes to word work.

Return, please, to figure 3.1 in the previous chapter (you'll be asked to do this often, for it is a critical organizer that will be useful in chapter after chapter). The layer of figure 3.1 presented here as figure 4.1 zooms in on the strategies that work well for narrative text. We'll delve into the various sections of the organizer—in both indirect and direct realms.

The key *indirect* methods are the self-selection/collection strategies. In the *direct* realm, these are the *general* word-learning strategies as well as *specific* instructional strategies. The focus in this chapter will be on some of the graphic organizer variants particularly good for narrative texts, as well as

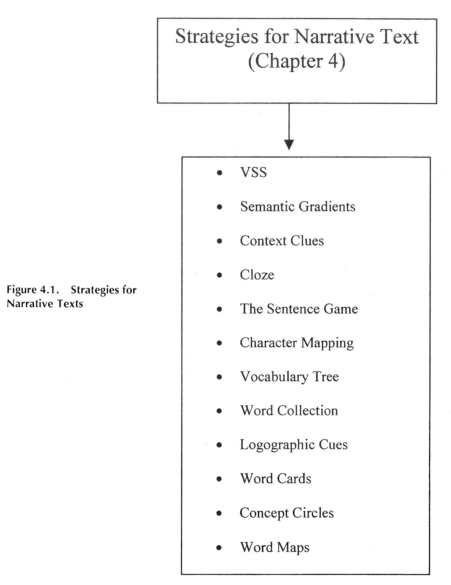

**Figure 4.1.   Strategies for
Narrative Texts**

concept circles, C(2)QU, story impressions, and Vocab-O-Grams. The other
specific instructional strategies will be presented in some detail in chapters 5
and 6. Two of the key *general* strategies, "tools" and "word parts/structural
analysis," get their own chapters (8 and 7, respectively).

CORE BOOKS

As with any approach, there are tradeoffs. The advantages of using core literature are as follows:

- All students read the same book—and it's usually "quality" literature.
- Parents like the consistency, for example, if it's district wide and a child changes buildings, the exposure is the same.
- Demonstration points/teachable moments are predictable.
- Preparation time and record keeping are pretty manageable.

The disadvantages are the following:

- No single title appeals to all children in a class.
- Readability is always a problem: given the range of students' reading skills in a typical classroom, a book will be too easy for some, too difficult for others.
- Grade to grade level articulation can be problematic.
- Alternative choices need to be available when a child has already read the book.

Think of vocabulary instruction as an aspect of word study, including both the teaching of word meanings and the teaching of sight vocabulary. Although there is a trend in some quarters toward decodable texts, in most literature-based situations students are bound to encounter words that are rich, complex, and previously either unknown or partially known. That's where good teaching comes in.

Even in the middle grades students learn a lot of vocabulary from books read aloud to them and from discussions. Through word walls and activities such as "making words" (Cunningham, 1995), English language learners (ELLs) learn labels for concepts, both novel and known. Vocabulary growth is also enhanced by the language experience approach. These are stories dictated by the students, with the teacher or an aide scribing in the students' exact words. This approach is appropriate for struggling readers and second language learners; examples of student work can be found in chapter 9. Wordless books are ideal organizers for language experience in heterogeneous groups, so that children hear the rich language, syntax, and vocabulary of others. It's funny how students who tend to tune the teacher out really pay attention to their peers.

In the intermediate grades and above, there are certain core word-learning strategies that are quite applicable and adaptable across grade levels.

Remember, they may be instructionally sound for informational text reading as well. If some of these are already in your instructional repertoires, tweak them, refine them. Be cautious about adding too many new ones too soon. With all of these strategies, the goal is to turn over responsibility to the student as soon as possible.

Harmon and Hedrick (2002) examined the question that often occurs in the middle level: what components in a literature-based program foster vocabulary growth? How variable and fluid are teacher beliefs—and how do they influence practice? Since trade books are the major instructional material used and since flexible grouping and self-selection often abound, how much variation is there? *And*, is it good?

Harmon and Hedrick (2002) enumerate ten recurring characteristics of literature-based classrooms, finding three major components:

1. instruction that expands schema
2. social interactions and interventions
3. wide reading

All three components promote active engagement with words via incidental learning as well as planned, deliberate instructional acts. The belief is that "skills" are learned and reinforced at the same time that students experience them. This means that the power of choice needs to be honored and that individual differences are respected—so that students make their own, personalized connections. Remember, too, that more organizational/instructional paths can be applied in order to maximize student learning.

Whole Class

During teacher-directed discussions, be sure to relate, explain, and specifically question your students—they will react, in turn, quite similarly by connecting and questioning. You as teacher must consistently establish "links" and common reference points. At times you'll need to get quite personal in order to help students grasp new words. Here is also where humor goes a long way. Additionally, the wise teacher "returns" the students to context, pointing out when it is, and also is not, useful.

You might, for example, show a sentence on the SMART Board or an overhead transparency: "Jules thought he had an air-tight *alibi*." Be clear that that context alone would be of little help in determining the meaning of the word "alibi." Then tell the students, "An *alibi* is an official story concerning where you were when something (usually) bad happened." Continue with synonyms and scenarios to help the kids gain a rich understanding of the word.

Provide short, concise definitions—they will be buttressed with extensions and clarifications. Clear, vivid examples help the words to stick:

> Have you ever seen an elderly person who has arthritis and his hands are all twisted? That's *gnarled*. Or have you ever seen a tree trunk that the trunk itself is twisted? That's *gnarled* as well.

This is an example of "text talking" (Beck & McKeown, 2001). Don't feel guilty about targeted telling as long as it is buttressed by other purposeful support. It's efficient, for it can be done by the whole class or in a group, as well as individually.

Students take their cues from the teacher, and their responses mirror the teacher's corrections, enthusiasm, and genuine curiosity. Due to purposeful repetition and reinforcement by the teacher, the students frequently *use* important new words in both oral and written formats.

Book Discussion Groups

Literature circles as described by Daniels (2002) are structured with defined roles, including "vocabulary enricher," also known as the "word wizard." Again, teacher behaviors that are modeled are evinced in their students. The vocabulary enrichers should rely on the dictionary as well as their peers as sources of word knowledge. Overall, students work collaboratively in these group sessions to construct meaning—sharing their insights and interpretations. The teacher moves among the groups, intervening occasionally, but largely facilitating and coaching.

Independent Reading

Students should keep personal logs, which afford opportunities for active use of strategies to "attack" new words as well as to reinforce words learned previously.

We know that students with the strongest vocabularies are usually the best readers and comprehenders. There is a good reason to share that information with your students, for knowing interesting words deeply is indicative of a smart person. Just about everybody recognizes the importance of wide reading *by* children. However, if students read only easy books, vocabulary growth is likely to be minimal! It's critical, then, to balance easy reading *by* students with some rich, challenging reading *to* students, coupled with text talking–type strategies.

Remember to involve the pupils in choosing "interesting words." In their zeal, conscientious teachers require students to look up and define lots of words, and often to memorize the definitions. Such work is often counterproductive! Remember, definitions do not ensure that a new word can actually be used. Students need to be actively engaged in vocabulary work in order for there to be any retention of any consequence.

Pearson and Johnson (1984) developed a very useful taxonomy of word relationships, presenting a categorical system of nine word relations in the following order: synonym, antonym, association, classification, analogy, connotation and denotation, multiple meaning, homograph, and homophones. For the first six of the nine (i.e., synonyms to connotative-denotative relationships), the "higher" level word-concept relationships subsume the thinking of the "lower." As an example, in order to do a word analogy, the understanding of synonym, antonym, association, and classification are all required. Obviously, the top three relations (multi-meaning, homograph, and homophone) occur only occasionally.

Now, finally, we can explore some direct and indirect vehicles for word learning. Remember, please, that these have been selected for inclusion in this chapter as being appropriate (more so) for narrative text as opposed to informational.

VOCABULARY SELF-COLLECTION STRATEGY (VSS)

VSS (Haggard, 1982) is deceptively simple, and was born out of necessity: students asked the ubiquitous question often pondered, sometimes raised, as to why they had to learn the words they were assigned. The teacher took a risk, scrapped the commercial curriculum, and had them each choose one word to

a. write on the board;
b. tell where it was found;
c. tell what (you) think it means; and
d. tell why (you) think the class should learn it.

The teacher contributed a word, too.

Over the years VSS has buttressed independent word learning via wide reading. It increases student ownership, motivation, and word awareness and reduces the limitations of traditional word instruction. Ruddell and Shearer (2002) conducted research on VSS and found strong support for it as an effective means to help students to become strategic, independent word learners. The word lists generated demonstrated that students consistently chose important, challenging words to learn.

A middle school developmental reading teacher adapted VSS to meet the needs of his students, particularly those who were reading self-selected texts. As opposed to the original VSS, where students were instructed to choose just one word, these students were looking for many new words. Students marked their chosen words lightly in pencil, directly in their texts. They were instructed *only* to mark the words at that time and to then go on with their reading. At the end of the chapter or at the end of an appropriate chunk, the students then revisited their chosen words. They were taught how to use ellipses, and they jotted down their words in partial context, this time on 4x11 inch strips of construction paper that served as bookmarks (see figure 4.2). At designated times they'd be asked to present their words for class discussion, or put some on the graffiti board (more on that later).

The bookmarks were turned in for credit when both sides were full. The words "owned" by the reader might then be added to a personal word bank, included in a word search, or put in an original crossword puzzle. Students need to understand that they need not write down every word they're not

---

Old Yeller by Fred Gipson

p1 ... his short hair was a dingy
   yellow ...
   (dirty-colored; not bright and
   clean)

p3 ... if you let the varmints eat up
   the roasting ears ... (dialect
   var. for vermin)

p6 ... cut a green mesquite sprout ...
   (thorny trees or shrubs)

p28 ... big chunks of chinking fell ...
   (not in dictionary)

p30 ... I'd had my appetite whetted ...
   (sharpened)

p31 ... the roan bull spilled ...
   (grayish-yellow; tawny)

p50 ... why, that old rogue ...
   (rascal; tramp)

p54 ... when the spotted heifer ...
   (a young cow)

p65 ... I was plenty scared of that
   hydrophobia plague
   (abnormal fear of water; rabies)

p32 ... she switched Arliss hard ...
   (to whip or beat)

-Here is a re-creation of what the bookmarks looked like.

-The students would turn in "full" bookmarks for extra credit points. At the end of the book, they'd have possibly seven or eight (or more) bookmarks stapled together.

-They'd put their words on the graffiti board, with definition included.

-They had the option to create either word searches or crossword puzzles using "their" words for classmates to solve. This act of going public was very motivating.

Figure 4.2. Bookmark

sure of. What you're trying to do is create the disposition for children to see themselves as word detectives, to be collectors of new and interesting words.

Students learn new words from ongoing and extended transactions with the words, their peers, and their teacher—all within the context of the classroom experience. Wide reading is a well-established means of acquiring vocabulary, but social and environmental influences should also be harnessed. Ruddell and Shearer (2002) conducted research that documented the growth of students as they engaged in the systematic use of VSS. Each student selected one word per week for study; the words could come from any source. In the "nomination process" the students were required to tell where their word was found, state what they thought it meant, and provide a rationale for why it merited inclusion on the list.

The VSS group scored significantly higher than controls in depth and breadth of vocabulary knowledge. Additionally, scrutiny of the VSS word lists demonstrated that when given the opportunity to select their words, the students consistently chose "important, interesting, challenging words to learn" (Ruddell & Shearer, 2002, p. 261). "VSS evidently jump-starts learners' linguistic-experiential capital; at-risk students suddenly become 'rich' with the capital necessary for academic success and are thereby able to add to their word knowledge base and their own effectiveness as learners" (p. 261).

The study results are clear about the critical importance of the teacher's role in guiding and mediating opportunities for students to benefit. It also reinforces the veracity of vocabulary learning that builds on language learning and peer talk in the classroom. Additionally, the notion that students will under-challenge themselves is debunked. Some teachers are quick to say, "Yeah, but my kids won't take it seriously." The rejoinder: they will if you will.

Remember, as with most of the strategies presented, the process can be modified to suit particular needs. As an example, if you are working with a flexible group or a small class, you can have the students bring two (or more) words to the table. You may also choose to have words from a particular content area, or that represent a theme, or that fall into a certain category in terms of part of speech (e.g., one week words must be adjectives). Whatever the variant activity, the basic steps are

- *select* (students bring own words),
- *present* (to the group),
- *vote* (on words to be learned),
- *extend* (and discuss—to elaborate on meanings),
- *enter* (into logs), and
- *extend further* (as you wish).

CONTEXT CLUES

As mentioned in chapter 3, context clues alone, at a single exposure, are just not very reliable. There are ways to *create* contexts, however, that are very supportive in a combination approach. For now, however, concentrate on naturally occurring context.

One definite problem with context clues is that they are often subtle and require a lot of inferring from readers. Second, context clues may give some readers some idea about the word's meaning, but that usually isn't sufficient for inferring specific meanings. Although context clues can sometimes give the gist of the meaning, they are usually not exact enough, rich enough, to allow students to define a word so that it is "transportable." Unless students own it and can use it independently in a variety of situations, it is not richly known.

Context clues have their limitations, but teachers still must teach about them, maximize their use, make the best of them. As students read and reread books, they develop increasingly sophisticated understandings of new word meanings, and begin to use these words in a variety of ways. And we do know that silent, personal reading is a rich source of incidental word learning. So a critical part of word learning happens when students have rich encounters with authentic texts. This type of informal learning can be enhanced by instruction that is thoughtful and explicit.

LAURA AT BEAVER CREEK

I was out in the field recently observing one of my reading practicum students, during a guided reading lesson with a group of four fourth graders. One of the children was reading orally in What's the Big Idea, Ben Franklin? *(Fritz, 1976) and ran into some trouble with the following passage—it was related to the notion of apprenticeships, and young Ben's father's notion that Ben should seek an alternative career path: "No, Mr. Franklin decided, he shouldn't. Benjamin would be a preacher. He'd go to Latin School, then he'd go to college, then he'd climb up into a* pulpit *and make his father proud" (p. 10).*

That little snippet is illustrative of the unreliability of naturally occurring context. When the young teacher-in-training stopped and asked the children what a "pulpit" was, three were clueless, and the fourth hazarded a guess: "some kind of chair." The clue from the word "preacher" was in the previous sentence, and the kids were probably absorbing the earlier conceptual challenge presented by the general word "apprenticeship" and new terms like "cooper" and "cutlerer,"

*that were also embedded in the previous context. After a brief explana-
tion of pulpit, they nodded their assent—it was a new word for them,
but conceptually concrete and easily incorporated in their vocabulary
banks—but repeated encounters would be needed.*

Teachers need to think aloud and model both the limitations and the contributions of the context to word learning. In rare cases, the context is quite
explicit about word meanings; at other times the clues the author gives offer
even a very bright student just "a whiff" of the meaning. Teachers need to be
intentional about exposing their students to various levels of context explicitness to develop sensitivity to the different levels of help context can provide.
Students need practice so that they know how to look for and use these clues.
Strategy sequences involve looking at the word and around the word, and
proposing and verifying meanings.

As far as instruction goes, have students collect examples of different
types of context clues. Conduct mini lessons, and try to stay away from work
sheets. Here are some examples to try:

- *Apposition* (a direct statement of a synonym or explanation): The tiara, *or
  crown*, was worn proudly by the princess.
- *What a word is not like*: *Unlike* the cheetah, a sloth moves very slowly.
  (This type requires students to understand signal words.)
- *What a word is used for*: Jimmy *used* the colander *to drain* the noodles.
- *Gist clues*: These are the most subtle clues that an author can offer her readers. With these clues, the meaning of a word must be inferred from the general context (or gist) of the passage. Sometimes the reader must read and
  reread far from the sentence containing the new word in order to understand
  the meaning. Here's an example of a gist passage from Beers (2003).

> John burst out of the woods and found himself at the edge of a precipice.
> Clinging to a boulder, he gazed down dizzily at the blue ribbon of river be-
> low. (p. 187)

In the above passage, the meaning of the word "precipice" is not directly
stated, nor is it in contrast with other words.

Once students have a basic sensitivity to some of the types of context clues,
they can be taught steps to help them know when and how to use them. For
example, Beers (2003) teaches middle level students to follow these steps:

1. *Stop.* Think. Recognize that a word is new or unknown to you.
2. *Check.* Are you pronouncing the word correctly? Are you sure the word is
   interfering with your understanding?

3. *Look*. Before and after the word.
4. *Reason*. Think what would make sense!
5. *Predict*. A possible meaning.
6. *Re-check*. Consult an expert, or look it up.

Teachers can also work with and prepare overheads or posters with Post-its, covering words, for a type of cloze activity.

Problem Solving with Context

According to McKeown (1985) the process involves several stages of active problem solving:

How and Why to Use Context

Students need to be instructed and moved incrementally along the continuum so that they understand the limitations and the possibilities of context in word learning. At times the clues given by the author are subtle, requiring a good deal of reading between and beyond the lines. At other times they are extremely explicit, are *right there*, readily apparent. Our students *need* to see the various levels of context explicitness—perhaps a continuum will help.

Kinds of Clues Provided by Context

Students need to develop an understanding of what context can and cannot do. They need to figure out what is transportable, what is likely to be really reliable.

How to Look For and Use This Information

This is most critical, of course. There are mini sequences that help students to learn what context can and cannot do for them. Although natural context is usually insufficient for deep and flexible word learning, *sometimes* it is just "right" and fits on the first exposure.

Some teachers have their students examine and collect different types of context clues. It's really powerful when the children share what they have found, and these make for perfect mini lessons. Rather than expecting students to absorb too much information about context clues, the teacher can control the information a bit. According to Blachowicz and Fisher (2010) one class "discovered" seven types of context clues. Following are their types:

1. *Synonyms*. The *apprentice*, the young person learning a trade, had to work for the silversmith for seven years.

2. *What a word is or is not like.* Maureen, unlike Seth, is very *liberal* in her pedagogy.
3. *Something about location or setting.* The *inductee* was blindfolded and had to wait alone outside the clubhouse.
4. *Something about what a word is for.* Biff used the *gig* to spear the sturgeon, but he had trouble fitting it through the hole in the ice.
5. *What kind of thing or action it is.* Skippy *taunted* his classmates, calling them nasty names.
6. *How something is done.* She *pirouetted*, then turned gracefully to the king.
7. *A general topic related to the words.* The sheriff tossed the bandits in the *hoosegow*.

Some Steps: Procedures to Teach Students

Students need structured group lessons to help them build and test hypotheses about word learning. One such sequence is the one presented by Beers (2003), which has been reduced down to four steps:

1. *Look.* Before and after the word; sometimes you'll need to go outside of the sentence containing the unknown.
2. *Reason.* Above all, think about what makes sense.
3. *Predict.* Give it your best shot, based on the practical information you have.
4. *Resolve or redo.* Are you satisfied with your answer? You need to be the judge as to whether your answer makes sense.

Remember, the three major types of word identification strategies (structural analysis, phonics, and context) are usually used in some combination by readers who encounter unfamiliar words in their reading. It is important to teach children to cross check the clues, repeatedly, until they have internalized the strategies.

Here is an example of the four-step process, with the emphasis on the "look" step—the teacher's emphasis is on getting the children to look beyond the sentence with the unknown.

The teacher makes a transparency with several sentences, covering all except this one: "They _____across the street."

Teacher: "What makes sense in this sentence?

Students: (To paraphrase, students say that there are many verbs that could make sense: walked, ran, strolled, hurried.)

Teacher: "With only the given sentence, we're not really sure what 'they' refers to. So, sometimes, in order to figure things out, we need to look beyond the sentence containing the word we don't know. Now, I'm going to show you the sentence that came before: "Skippy dropped the can of tennis balls. They _____across the street."

"Now what would fit?"

Students: (Paraphrasing, they recognize that the pronoun "they" refers to the tennis balls, and they decide that *bounced* or *rolled* are two possible answers, but they can't be sure without some phonetic information.)

To recapitulate, the teacher creates a transparency with a key word either omitted or highlighted. Then students are walked through the previously mentioned steps:

- *look*
- *reason*
- *predict*
- *resolve or redo*

What's critical is the discussion, the revealing of the thinking process, the reasoning.

Here's another example:

Teacher's overhead has this sentence: "The Bucks *decimated* the Pistons . . ."

Teacher: "What does the word 'decimated' mean?"

Students: (Paraphrasing, the students realize it could mean "played," but they think it means "beat." They decide that it would be what the Bucks did to the Pistons, so that "lost" would not make sense.)

Teacher: "So you *reasoned* and *predicted*. Now let's look at a little bit more information so that you guys can *redo* your prediction if necessary": "The Bucks *decimated* the Pistons, 122–80."

Students: (The students then redo their predictions, having inferred that the word "decimated" means "destroyed" or "beat badly.")

The use of context clues can be done in a very game-like fashion, as well as cooperatively. The teacher can create word cards with unknowns "blanked out," and students can be taught to do the same. Students are taught to try to take full advantage of the context, but that it may be necessary to go beyond the context for information, when not enough information is provided—that is, go to the dictionary, or ask someone.

THE CLOZE PROCEDURE

Although the cloze procedure has been around for a long time, it certainly has its utility, for it requires that students use context to infer word meanings. It is flexible, and can be used with individuals, small groups, or the whole class. When cloze passages are used for assessment, every fifth word is typically removed. However, when cloze is used for instruction, it can be customized and tweaked to meet the needs of individual children.

> As middle school students _____ toward independence in managing _____, it only makes sense _____ give them more and more ___ _____. I would like to _____ some instructional ideas to _____ teachers to help these_____. Although the ideas have _____ specifically applied with seventh _____ students, they can certainly ____ _____ adapted to be used _____ other grade levels.

Some practitioners say that only the exact word from the original passage should be counted as "correct," but it is preferable to have students supply sets of words that might create a meaningful passage. So in the above case, you might have the following:

> As middle school students *move/progress* toward independence in managing *reading/learning*, it only makes sense to give them more and more *trust/freedom/responsibility*. I would like to *share* some instructional ideas to *help* teachers to help these *students*. Although these ideas have *been* specifically applied with seventh *grade* students they can certainly *be* adapted to be used *at* other grade levels.

It is interesting that the "structure" words (often called the glue words, the high-frequency, recurring words like "of," "the," "be," "is," and so forth) are not as readily substituted for as are the content words.

In addition to the more basic varieties of the cloze procedure, this chapter will touch briefly on subcategories: oral cloze, zip cloze, choice cloze, and synonym cloze (Blachowicz & Fisher, 2010).

Oral Cloze

Oral cloze can be used for ELLs, or for any students who are struggling with oral language. The key, as you can imagine, revolves around rich language use as students explain their reasoning. A "picture walk" is a good way to start out, to activate prior knowledge, and when appropriate to point out pictures that support the construction of meaning. The teacher may also choose to read aloud, substituting a "beep" for each of the words omitted. Teachers should choose the text carefully, honing in on high interest, natural language, and predictability. Don't forget the importance of capturing illustrations and familiar experiences. It's a great strategy for helping children cross check and make full use of multiple cues.

In oral cloze, children need to focus and to store information. As the teacher, or a designated student, reads the passage, the students supply possibilities for the words omitted. The surrounding context is, of course, a key consideration. The procedure helps the students to develop a sense of flexibility, as they listen to their peers and come to realize the range of words that may "fit."

Even though middle level students are typically not yet interested in automobile insurance, they are probably familiar with the Geico Gecko, the pitchman (or pitchreptile) on television ads.

> Of course, what the _____ lacks in _____, he actually makes up for in savings for his customers. The fact is _____ has been helping people save _____ for over seventy _____.

This example should be completed orally. Offer the students the opportunity to reveal their thinking. It can be done with or without a word box.

Zip Cloze

This strategy helps the students by providing constant feedback to encourage them to persevere when, for example, context clues alone are not rich enough to supply the needed meaning. Whereas a strong reader will push on in an effort to make meaning when there is a breakdown, a less able reader often becomes frustrated and either gives up or asks for help.

The preferred method is to put the passage on an overhead transparency or the SMART Board. Have the children skim in order to get an overview of the general meaning. Then go to the masked words, and as the teachers "zips" off the masking tape or Post-its, the students get a great deal of immediate feedback.

Students enjoy preparing zip selections for their peers. A hybrid that is very successful for older students is to have them black out selected words from newspaper selections:

> Whether he gets the sack or not, Flanigan creates _____ and disrupts every play.

In this example, the targeted word is "mayhem." The teacher might choose to cater to the interests of young male readers by having them explain the specialized use of "sack" in the sentence.

Additional scaffolding can be given by providing strategic letters or clues as to word length.

The _ m _ is a flightless _ _ _ _.
The _ _ _ _ _ _ _ _ _ _ is a flightless _ _ _ _.

Choice Cloze

This form of cloze provides needier students with added support. As opposed to deleting words in a passage, the teacher creates choices from which the students select. The teacher should be sure to make the choices clear—with a very definite best answer. Here are some examples:

illegal
Andy was sitting in a *comfortable* chair.
charming

stars
The night sky was full of *stairs*.
stares

This variation does require some teacher time for preparation. It is good for helping students with tracking difficulties, and it provides a bridge that requires students to judge contextual appropriateness without having to generate their own answers. Additionally, children can focus on meaning without having to devote attention to conventional spelling. A notable exception, however, would be the second example, with "stars, stairs, stares"—the teacher chose two homophones and a word that is "close" enough to be easily confused. Children solving that item clearly need to pay attention to overlapping spelling and meaning conventions—but they don't need to *generate* the information.

Synonym Cloze

This is another variant that provides cues, a support system until students are ready to do the full cloze procedure. Words are omitted, but a synonym or phrase is provided in order to help the student.

Nathaniel found a _____ that had fallen from the nest.
baby bird

There are several possibilities here: some extra graphophonic clues can be provided; a word box can be used; or, vocabulary can be pre-introduced.

Nathaniel found a *fl*_____ that had fallen from the nest.
　　　　　　　　　baby bird

It is also possible to do this with antonyms, but that can be complicated, depending on the explicitness and on the child.

Nathaniel found a *friendly* puppy.
　　　　　　　　vicious

This section has dealt with various ways to "present" context clues, which are transportable and generalizable to all aspects of vocabulary learning, as outlined in figure 3.1.

Before we launch deeper into contextual activities and strategies that interplay with making meaning in narrative reading, remember that in order to attain most readers' goals, some margin for error exists: that is, there can be typically an unknown word (or two, or three) per page and the child can still "understand" the story. Please note my earlier description regarding strategies vis-à-vis activities, and refer to the master list. A quick revisit to figures 3.1 and 4.1 will help to situate these for you. These are included in this chapter due to their "best fit" with narrative reading, but some certainly would also be of high utility in informational reading.

SPECIFIC STRATEGIES FOR NARRATIVE TEXT

The Sentence Game

This strategy (Barr & Johnson, 1990) requires the teacher to prepare a question and a three-sentence context for each word. Obviously, this is pretty "expensive" in terms of preparation and later engagement by the student, so it is important that words of high salience and utility are selected. At any rate, here are the steps:

First, devise a question centered on the key word.
Then, a broad context.
Then, more detailed information.
Then, an explicit definition.

Here is an example:

Question: What does a herpetologist do?
Sentence 1: The herpetologist was hired by the zoo.
Sentence 2: The herpetologist "milked" the poison from the king cobra.
Sentence 3: A herpetologist studies snakes.

The game is played, according to Barr and Johnson (1990), following this format. Student teams are shown the question and sentence 1 only. If a team can answer the question after only the first sentence is presented, two points are awarded. If the second sentence is needed, then one point is earned. Finally, sentence 3 is needed only if the word is unknown—it is then used for teaching purposes. Games can be very motivating for many pupils, and certainly provide variety.

Character Mapping and Other Graphic Organizers

Mapping of words is a common strategy in many classrooms. It is quite useful as a pre-reading activity, for sharing relationships among words. It does not take a lot of preparation time, and is great for keeping students engaged. Mapping can also be useful as a post-reading activity or assessment. The focus right now is on mapping varieties that are useful for teaching and/or reinforcing vocabulary in narrative text.

Character development is a central component of any literature for children or adults, and any measures to aid understanding of the author's craft can be very useful. In character maps, characters are described, using the author's words or the children's words, and answers are supported by the text.

It is preferable to do these on butcher paper, as opposed to a chalkboard that needs to be erased. These character maps can then be built upon incrementally and saved indefinitely as the reading of a piece unfolds over days, and even weeks. The teacher should do the big map, and students keep their own copies. An example for *Lord of the Flies* appears in figure 4.3.

Have the students use different colors at different junctures of their reading. In the example in figure 4.3, students might "stop and jot" (see chapter 6) with the describing characteristics already filled in. Another option is to fill in the page numbers that help to locate the passages that support certain characteristics.

Vocabulary Trees

This type of organizer overlaps with chapter 7, regarding structural analysis, roots, and affixes. Building vocabulary trees is much more engaging than

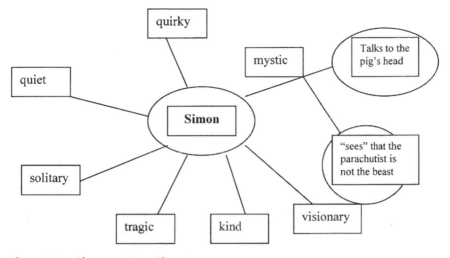

Figure 4.3. Character Map (Simon)

simply giving students lists of roots with their definitions and examples. Students and teachers can initially "grow" a few of their trees together, and then students can make their own.

To grow such a tree, you (or they) choose a root word to study and write it at the root of the tree. Under the root, write the definition. In figure 4.4 the root is "vac" with the definition "empty" written below it. In the trunk, the students then write a key word—one that they all know—and add a definition. Then, in the branches, students add as many other words as they can. As their skills and teacher comfort dictate, they may add the context in which they found the words as well as the source.

Again, students can build their trees over time, add to them, and periodically share them or turn them in.

Word Collection

Creative teachers find things to "do" with words that students self-select. They want their students to truly engage with words, old and new. And they understand the need for repetition until the words become automatic. The key is some form of VSS, usually the bookmark. The words are then used in the following ways, some aforementioned:

- Put the words on the graffiti board.
- Use the words to construct word searches or crossword puzzles to be solved by peers.

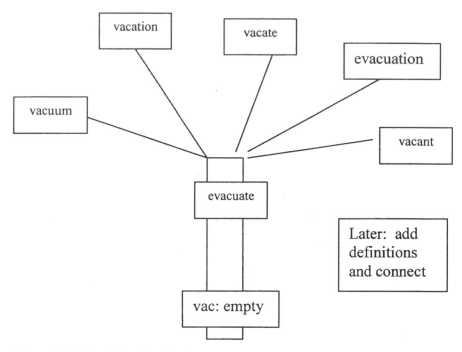

Figure 4.4. Vocabulary Tree (vac)

- Put the words on 3 × 5 cards: in isolation on one side, in context on the other side.
- Use the 3 × 5 cards repeatedly—for sorting, on the word wall, for Shazam!

For Shazam! several players dump equal amounts of "their" words into a box or some similar container. Mixed in among the word cards are Shazam! cards, at about a 1:10 ratio. Students pass the container and draw a card. If they pronounce and define the word correctly, they keep it. If they give a wrong answer, they return the card to the pool; if, however, they get a Shazam! card they must return *all* of their cards (the game is usually played to a total of seven cards). This ensures that plenty of attention is paid by those students who are not actually taking their turn. The game is motivating and requires focus and concentration. Students grow to see the power of repetition, as words become more and more automatic.

Logographic Cues

Children enjoy creating logographs, which help them better understand vocabulary words. On one side of the card, students write the vocabulary word;

on the other side, they write the definition and draw a logograph that keys the meaning of the word. A vocabulary logograph can be anything that helps a student remember the meaning of a word—this will vary from student to student, as it's quite personal. For example, some students create logographs to help them remember where they originally saw the word.

Logographs can act as a powerful scaffold to bolster word knowledge, which in turn increases comprehension—always our ultimate goal for developing readers. As students decide how to visually present a key idea in the text, they are, of course, encouraged to think critically about what they are reading. So, a logograph is simply a visual symbol, designed to offer the reader a high-utility message in a minimum amount of space.

Concept Circles

Concept circles (Vacca & Vacca, 2001) are another versatile, flexible tool that can be applied across grade levels, to either content areas or to narrative text. Students are provided another format to relate words conceptually to one another. Concept circles are very much like analogies. We typically divide a circle into four sections, and start off putting words in all sections, directing the students to describe the relationship among the sections.

In figure 4.5a, all four terms are related because they describe temperature. The teacher provided all four parts, and the students filled in the category. An adaptation would be to provide all four sections, and have students circle or shade in the section that does not fit. In figure 4.5b, three are temperature words, and the emotion word would be taken out. In the next example, the teacher provides three words, and the students fill in the fourth when they have figured out the concept relationship. In figure 4.5c, any emotion word is a defensible answer, but a more precise answer would be to ascertain that they are all "positive" emotions, and that a word such as "elated" would be a better answer than "sad," for example. Of course, teachers can leave two or three blanks, and the object is to soon turn over the creation of the concept

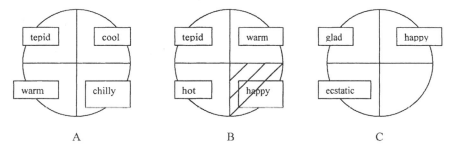

| A | B | C |

Figure 4.5. Concept Circles

Figure 4.6.   Concept Circles

circles to the students. Discussing and defending answers and elaborating on their reasoning are very, very important.

In figure 4.6a, the teacher supplies only Mississippi, and students would supply, possibly, three other states, or states that start with M (Maine, Montana, Missouri) or southern states. Answers will vary, but it is the articulation of the reasoning that matters. In figure 4.6b, Mississippi and Amazon are supplied, which requires the students to find another meaning for Mississippi, in this case the river. In figure 4.6c, we have a possible analogy-type relationship. In this case, if students have the prior knowledge, they could fill in the two blanks with any two characters by Sir Arthur Conan Doyle, or they can parallel the hero and sidekick relationship, adding "Lone Ranger" and "Tonto" or "Batman" and "Robin."

Word Cards

These cards today are much more instructionally sound than simple flash cards. They provide several reinforcers for associating words and their definitions with "triggers" from a student's personal experience. These cards can be tweaked so that they contain antonyms as well as synonyms, and the words can be presented both in and out of context.

In figure 4.7, Jared has the key word "obstreperous" cued by the association with Tyron, a character in a short story who Jared finds to be defiant and unruly. Try to keep word cards succinct and straightforward. On the reverse side write the word in context along with antonyms and possible analogies.

As students collect their personal vocabulary cards, they can use them for the creation of word puzzles to share with their classmates, or to "go public" in other ways.

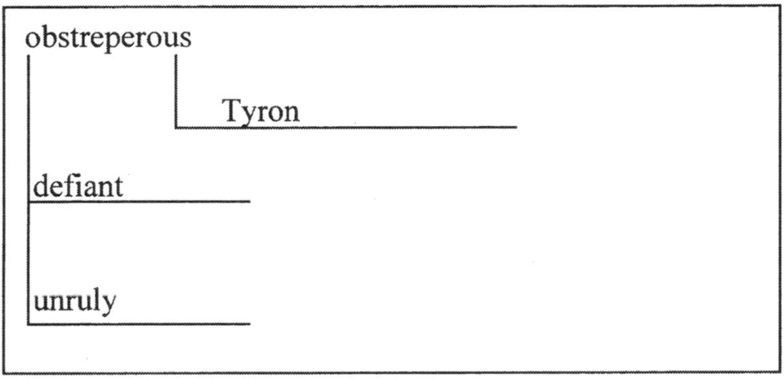

```
obstreperous
                  Tyron

defiant

unruly
```

Figure 4.7. Word Card (Tyron)

Word Maps

According to Schwartz and Raphael (1985), this technique is useful for help-ing students develop a general sense of what constitutes a definition. Children are made aware of the types of information that comprise a definition, as well as how that information is organized. The word map model has answers to three questions: What is it? What is it like? What are some examples? Green-wood (2003) used the organizer found in figure 4.9.

Physical therapists are usually highly trained. Generally speaking they specialize in helping people with physical problems (e.g., after being in a cast for a broken leg for two months, Crystal saw a physical therapist who set up a program for her).

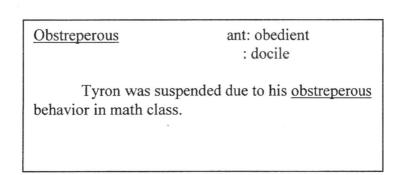

Figure 4.8. Word Card (obstreperous)

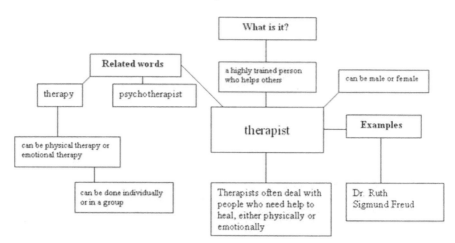

Figure 4.9.   Word Map (therapist)

Or, Crystal may need to talk to a family therapist about the problems at home.

In this manner, the general term is dealt with first—the students then delve into specifics.

Vocab-O-Gram

The Vocab-O-Gram strategy (Blachowicz & Fisher, 2010) focuses on vocabulary to learn the elements of story, variously, setting, character(s), problem, and solution. It's a highly motivating way for students to learn vocabulary *and* story elements.

- Choose your text, then pull out ten to fifteen words that relate to the story events (often called story elements).
- Divide the class into small groups, ranging from two to four in number. Assign a recorder for each group.
- Hand out the blank Vocab-O-Gram to each group. Clarify that they are to group the words given in the left hand boxes, and to use those words to explain their predictions in sentences in the right column.
- Allow plenty of time for the students to discuss the words and to place them on the chart.
- Invite students to share their ideas and reasoning.
- Read the text aloud.

- Have students return to their groups to adjust and revise—provide a different colored pen or pencil.
- Follow up, repeat as necessary, with strugglers.

Dana is a fourth grade teacher who is preparing to do a mythology unit with her class. She pulls fourteen good words from *The Face in the Pool: The Story of Echo and Narcissus* (Osbourne, 1989).

flower	love	mountain
boy	cruel	beautiful
forest	pool	embrace
king	Queen	cave
tears	echo	

Dana also tweaked the Vocab-O-Gram sheet provided by Blachowicz and Fisher (2010), simplifying it to meet her students' need.

Story Impressions

This technique (McGinley & Denner, 1987) calls on students to read a set of words (quickly!) and to get some impression about various story elements—the students then write their own versions before reading. It results in a rather elaborate prediction for the students to confirm or disconfirm.

Before reading "Young Percival," an Arthurian legend, fifth graders are given these words, preselected by Miss Sabolito:

England	knights	King Arthur
killed	determined	
Percival	peasant	
imagination	enemy	

Fifth graders Melissa and Kathy write,

Long ago in *England*, *King Arthur* ruled Camelot. One day a dreadful dragon, attacked, and *killed* two of Arthur's best *knights*. Arthur was *determined* to get revenge. With the help of Merlin's *imagination*, his solution was to have a *peasant* boy named *Percival* slay the dragon, the *enemy* of his kingdom.

Melissa and Kathy clearly have background knowledge, which they tap, even pulling Merlin into their plot. They have a setting, characters, a problem, and a solution.

The groups would then briefly share their "impressions" (don't overkill here!) and then get on with their reading. Here are the story impression steps (McGinley & Denner, 1987):

1. Teacher chooses vocabulary related to story grammar and displays it on the overhead, chalkboard, or chart paper.
2. Students then write a brief story using the words.
3. Share, compare, and contrast *before* reading text/passage.
4. Read the selection.
5. After reading, refine vocabulary as necessary.

Don't follow the steps slavishly—for example, this can be an individual stop and jot–type activity.

Knowledge Rating

Although at times self-report data can be inaccurate whether it comes from students or adults, it still can be very useful. The process is somewhat akin to others in this chapter. In this case, vocabulary is previewed, best guesses as to meaning are made, and students read actively and gather information to confirm or disconfirm, or refine, their original conjectures (Blachowicz, 1986).

Let's say that students are about to read a selection on the 1960s. The Knowledge Rating sheet shown in figure 4.10 would be used to start.

Knowledge ratings can be done individually, shared in small groups, then in large groups. It is important that children feel comfortable revealing what they don't know—make it clear that it's only prior knowledge (students should be reminded that the teacher may lack prior knowledge about many topics). Then have students make predictions about terms that are still unclear.

Term, Name	Can Define/Use	Heard It	Don't Know It
hippie			
draft dodging			
protest			
assassination			
acid			

Figure 4.10.   Knowledge Rating—1960s

Context Puzzles

This strategy fits two places in this book, for it certainly relates to the use of context clues. Going back to the underpinnings discussed earlier, a single exposure to a word is rarely enough, no matter how salient the word or concept—and typically, many reinforcers are necessary. This strategy provides lots of reinforcement, in a sort of double cloze activity, for students must really attend at the word level as well as at the sentence level.

The puzzle format helps to motivate youngsters. Remember that this is a reinforcer of previously introduced vocabulary.

d __ __ p i __ __
a __ __ __ u __ __ __ i c
c __ __ __ r __ __
i __ t __ __ r __ __
__ __ n g __ __ __

Bill grew to *despise* his former boss.
His intentions were _____, for he was always doing good deeds
    to help others.
The wounded animal _____ in fear.
Jamaal is an _____ part of the team.
The pit bull _____ the man's leg.

These are great for spelling. If you choose to use a word box, for variety include the definition, not the word.

Semantic Gradients

This strategy coupled with follow-up activities requires that children know words very well and be able to discern shades of meaning. Its effectiveness lies in the interconnectedness with other known words. In traditional vocabulary activities, so often teachers are satisfied when students memorize and regurgitate a simple, shallow definition or synonyms or antonyms. The semantic gradient takes the enterprise to another level.

As an example, in a commercial package for sixth graders, the word "amateur" is in the anthology, and the publisher makes the decision that it is a word that merits instruction. So included in the package are black line masters and workbook pages that include "amateur" as a worthy word—and define it as "one who does something unskillfully." Similarly, antonyms and synonyms are given. Olympic athletes are mostly amateurs! Think back to the gymnast Paul Hamm in Athens in 2004—he was an amateur, but he was far from "unskillful." It's easier to define words narrowly, but it's not reflective of the complexity and richness of language.

Strictly speaking, two different words cannot truly be synonyms, although they might be close. A semantic gradient requires students to make connections between known words and new vocabulary—which is a pedagogically sound principle that undergirds vocabulary (and other) instruction. Also sound is the arrangement in a graphic form. Encourage students to array the words in a pocket chart, or on strips with magnets, so that they can manipulate them. Again, discussion and defending reasoning are very important. Teachers can start off by supplying all the words to be arrayed, but gradually students should be involved in generating words to add to the list.

Two examples follow: Students are asked to arrange the first group from most happy to angriest, and the second list from most overweight to leanest:

livid	_____	gaunt	_____
furious	_____	cadaverous	_____
glad	_____	obese	_____
elated	_____	trim	_____
upset	_____	corpulent	_____
ecstatic	_____	slender	_____
mad	_____	average	_____
indifferent	_____	chubby	_____
happy	_____	thin	_____

Blachowicz and Fisher (2010) present an example with gradations related to temperature. These authors make a good point, noting that "[t]hey can also expand their list to include other words related to temperature (e.g., steamy, scorching, raw, balmy, and glacial). What they will discover is that some of the words generated apply only in particular instances. For example, a day can be 'balmy,' but a dinner cannot" (p. 96).

Remember that semantic gradients can clarify distinctions among some words, but they may not be neatly applied to all word relationships. Greenwood and Flanigan (2007) developed an overlapping strategy that combined context clues with semantic gradients. Additionally, Greenwood (in press) triangulated the complementary strategies, adding PAVE work (a form of active dictionary use for cross-checking and confirming) to the use of context clues.

C(2)QU

The purpose of C(2)QU (Blachowicz, 1993) is to use context at the same time that specific vocabulary is presented. So definition and contextual information allow students to hypothesize about meaning and articulate the cues. This procedure takes some preparation time, but it compensates for the fact that "natural" context is often not rich enough for a word to be truly learned. The steps are as follows, as outlined by Blachowicz:

1. Present the word in a broad but meaningful context.
2. Provide more explicit context, including some definitional information.
3. Ask a question that involves semantic interpretation of the word.
4. Ask the students to use the word in a meaningful sentence.

An example of C(2)QU follows. This is another pretty formulaic strategy, somewhat similar to the sentence game:

C1 (first example in *context*)
C2 (second example in *context*)
Q (*question* involving interpretation)
U (students *use* the word in a meaningful sentence)

Again, it's expensive time-wise, so you as teacher must be judicious:

C1 The hobo moved into a *hovel*.
C2 The hobo's *hovel* leaked rain, had no electricity, and no heat.
Q Would a wealthy person by likely to live in a *hovel*?
U (Teacher and students to use word in a meaningful sentence, or to give attributes.)

The two strategies presented here are also useful for informational text reading and vocabulary learning. Remember, as teacher, to model flexibility for your students.

C1 John was faced with a rather pleasant *dilemma*. (first example in *context*)
C2 John's *dilemma* related to his indecision about which of the two lucrative job offers he should accept. (second example in *context*)
Q Can a *dilemma* be a choice between two unequal alternatives? Can two alternatives ever be exactly equal? (*question* open to interpretation)
U (The teacher then asks students to *use* the targeted word, possibly relating the term to a personal occurrence.)

Dilemma is a word that students can easily relate to. It could be presented before, during, or after reading, say, Frank Stockton's famous short story "The

Lady or the Tiger." According to Blachowicz and Fisher (2010), C(2)QU is also a good process for cooperative reading groups when an assigned role is that of vocabulary director or word wizard.

Three Word Wonders

This activity is similar to concept circles and analogies. Simply give the students three words and have them be as precise as possible in giving the category to which all three words belong. These can be presented either orally or in written form. When done orally, they definitely promote good listening skills. As you will see, they also promote flexibility and divergent thinking. They are good for all content areas, as well as pop culture.

As always, discussion is critical. First you "take off the top of your head," explaining your thinking. For instance, when you hear or read "Columbus" you are thinking state capitals or explorers. Paired with "Hudson" you are still thinking explorers, you discard state capitals, but you add the possibility of rivers. "Drake seals it," you say. "It has to be explorers."

Here are several examples:

smog	mohawk	sawtooth	tennis
motel	buzz	tetan	badminton
chunnel	mullet	pocono	squash
(word blends)	(hairstyles)	(mountains)	(racket sports)

See appendix 2-D for more.

However these strategies are organized and reorganized, there are going to be misfits and overlaps. As we get ready to deal with the directly instructed methods for (mainly) expository text, be sure to resist the temptation to layer in too much, too soon! There are many good strategies out there, plus motivation and individual factors to consider. You need to give your students both variety and structure.

Chapter Five

Teaching Vocabulary in the Content Areas

We don't actually have to do much to make words matter to our students. They know the power of words. They know that words shape and define, hurt and shame, anger and bruise, soothe and comfort, encourage and mend. . . . They know that words give them access or deny them entry.

—Kylene Beers, in *Voices from the Middle*

DAVID

I work as a research assistant on a study funded by the National Institute of Justice—our team is investigating the incidence of learning deficiencies in incarcerated adults. Graterford is one of nine prisons in three states (Pennsylvania, Louisiana, and Washington) in which we are working.

I work with David, who was chosen at random (and consented) to participate in the study. He is black; I am white. We graduated from high school the same year—he from an urban school; me, suburban. He went to Vietnam; I went to a small liberal arts college where I played basketball and majored in English. He developed a drug habit while in 'Nam and came home to no job. At about the same time that I got my first teaching job, he participated in a liquor store robbery. His partner killed a clerk, and David is serving a life sentence.

David talks to me about the courses that are offered to him while he is in "the joint." He points out that the younger inmates serving shorter sentences get priority—the thinking being that they will be back on the streets sooner.

He is extremely articulate. As we get to know each other, we talk about how he developed those skills.

> *Scott, I read all the time now. But it sure wasn't from those workbooks they used in the courses here. List after list. Abominable, aviary, arcane. . . . That's what most of those words were, arcane. And useless. But going to the library and reading things of interest to me was very fulfilling. I just wish I had read when I was a kid.*

David and I corresponded for several years after the research ended, then we lost touch. He is probably still serving time in that grim, dangerous, depressing cage that we call a penitentiary. Penitent. Penance. Had he grown up in my environment—read to at home, attending reasonably safe, good schools—(and vice versa), our life situations could easily have been reversed.

In the previous chapter, the focus was on vocabulary learning from (and for) reading literature. Remember, a reader can accomplish her goals for reading narrative text without knowing every word on the page. Whereas many of the strategies introduced in chapter 4 are quickly turned over to the students, some of the strategies in this chapter require a lot of teacher planning, and a great deal of teacher direction. Control should be turned over to students very carefully, cautiously.

Please examine figure 5.1, which presents the informational text strategies. The previously mentioned direct and indirect methodologies certainly impact content area reading, and there are clearly overlaps. The focus of this chapter will be on specific word instruction. These strategies are intended for use with technical vocabulary, words that are central to the understanding of important concepts.

WHICH WORDS SHOULD BE TAUGHT

In earlier chapters the point has been made that

- word knowledge is critical to comprehension;
- wide reading must be encouraged and facilitated, for thousands of words are learned naturally through wide reading and oral communication.

Now comes a third guideline. Teachers need to use direct instruction to teach passage-critical words. Passage-critical words are words the teacher deems essential to understanding a text when the text provides insufficient

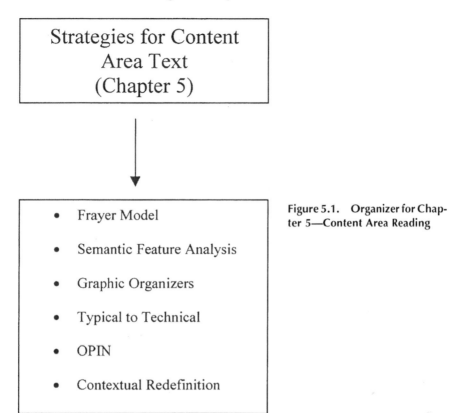

Figure 5.1. Organizer for Chapter 5—Content Area Reading

clues to enable the reader to infer the meaning. These passage-critical words often occur in the content areas.

The report of the National Research Council (Snow, Burns, & Griffin, 1998) examined the research and put it quite simply: "Vocabulary instruction does result in measurable increases in students' specific word knowledge" (p. 217). When teachers explain exactly what students are expected to learn and demonstrate the steps necessary, students learn more.

As children begin to learn vocabulary for the content areas, they encounter more and more words—some are new words for previously existing concepts, whereas others represent new concepts as well. Additionally, previously partially known concepts are expanded and built upon.

DRIVING NATHANIEL

This morning I am driving my six-year-old to kindergarten. Nathaniel is bright and cheery, talkative and inquisitive. I tell him that yesterday I

found a large snapping turtle that had been run over by a car. I picked
it up, took it home, and buried it in the leaves near the house so that
Nathaniel would eventually have another turtle shell for his collection.
I tell him I put it under the leaves in order for it to "decompose." He
immediately asks me what decompose means. I explain to him how the
flesh will "rot away," how maggots eat away at the turtle's carcass
until only the shell is left. He listens carefully, nods in understanding.

He had the concept of rotting down pat. I reinforced it. And "decom-
pose" was simply a new term for a previously existing concept.

When teaching in the content areas, the demands for deep and precise word knowledge require excellent direct teaching. In narrative reading and writing instruction, many times a child may only reach a superficial knowledge of the meaning of a word; it may not be important for a student to remember the meaning of the word after reading the book. And in writing, a student may need to know only a particular meaning to use a word effectively.

In contrast, in the content areas, certain words and concepts are central to understanding an entire topic. In some cases, subsequent instruction may hinge on retention of fairly sophisticated understanding of previously introduced terms and concepts.

"Knowing" a word is a continuous process. Remind your students that adults constantly refine and extend their knowledge of a word's meanings through different encounters with the word. In the same manner, students in the content areas both learn new terms and concepts *and* refine and extend their word knowledge.

TEACHING NEW WORDS AND NEW CONCEPTS

Many researchers cite evidence that vocabulary growth comes from extensive experience reading and being read to (Beck, McKeown, & Kucan, 2002). Some scholars even argue that exposure to print influences vocabulary growth more than everyday language experiences (Stanovich, 1986). Print exposes students to more complex language, new concepts for known words, new words, and new ideas. Although many struggling readers eventually master decoding processes, their language deficits can reappear if

- they do not know what words mean when they say or hear them;
- the conceptual level of texts is too complex, that is, the language is obtuse and there are too many unknowns;
- they lack inferential skills or have gaps in background knowledge.

As these children move on through the grades, negotiating the more complex syntax and abstract ideas in content area textbooks presents new obstacles for them (Baker, Simmons, & Kameenui, 1995). Teachers in the elementary grades, particularly at the primary level, guide their students through narrative text that is many times carefully leveled. When they hit the "read to learn" stage, teachers and children are often stymied.

PRACTICUM

Today I am out in the public schools with my undergraduate reading practicum students. In a fourth grade class, I see some children reading easy text independently, and others being guided through text that is a wee bit of a stretch through careful teacher scaffolding. Many of those youngsters at both extremes (i.e., some of both categories) will be ticketed for trouble when they hit reading requirements for social studies and science over the next few years. They may encounter content area teachers whose philosophy is "I'm here to teach, they're here to learn."

Remember, the National Reading Panel (NRP, 2000) reported that direct instruction of vocabulary improved students' reading comprehension. On the other hand, the NRP did not find compelling evidence that programs that are designed to increase students' independent reading promoted vocabulary growth. Although scholars can make some generalizations about the characteristics of effective vocabulary instruction, the number of studies that have directly examined the effects of vocabulary instruction on reading comprehension is still relatively small.

The solution of the tension between direct instruction and immersion/wide reading should be pretty apparent: the teacher needs the ability to make efficient use of vocabulary instruction, particularly in the content areas. He must identify the words and concepts that are likely to pose serious problems for the students, and then figure out the time-cost issues. Different professions have specialized vocabulary that separates them from others. Think of lawyers, doctors, accountants, scientists—they all use specialized language. Here is an excerpt of a letter written by an "insider" to another:

> Initial manifestations consisted of right-sided bradykenesia, gait impairment, and depression. Treatment was initiated with selegiline with subsequent introductions of pramipexole, and levodopa. His medical picture is otherwise complicated by a traumatic left radial nerve laceration which has been addressed by a host of tendon transposition procedures and intermittent botulinum toxin treatments to relieve muscular hypertonicity.

Even a well-read adult would have significant difficulty comprehending the passage due to the specialized vocabulary. There are probably too many unknowns included for the reader to use context clues well enough. Imagine how a struggling middle level student feels when confronted with the passages of "grade level" text.

By taking into account the goals of a lesson, the amount of teaching time required and depth of knowledge a word would require, and when in the lesson it would be most profitable to explore the word, Flanigan and Greenwood (2007) arrived at a four-level structure, as opposed to the three-tier model offered by Beck, McKeown, and Kucan (2002). In some cases, comprehension of a text depends on sophisticated knowledge of specific words that may be unfamiliar to some (or many) of the students. Teachers must choose the words that merit intensive instruction very carefully. Following are some strategies that work well for teaching words intensively.

The Frayer Model

This is an old and reliable word study method, and it provides a thorough basis for understanding new words. It is also rather complex and can be quite time consuming. It was mentioned briefly in chapter 2; now we'll delve more deeply. It is justifiable to spend the required time only if the concept is central to the work in the classroom. Frayer and her colleagues (Frayer, Frederick, & Klausmeiser, 1969) originally outlined a seven-step procedure.

1. Define the new concept, discriminating the attributes relevant to all instances of the concept.
2. Discriminate the relevant from the irrelevant properties of the concept.
3. Provide an example of the concept.
4. Provide a non-example of the concept.
5. Relate the concept to a subordinate concept.
6. Relate the concept to a superordinate concept.
7. Relate the concept to a coordinate term.

All seven steps (Frayer et al., 1969) (in lockstep) do not always "fit" real well, depending on the new concept teachers are working with. Steps 2, 3, and 4 are most critical, and you should focus on relevant versus irrelevant properties and examples versus non-examples. *Then* arrive at the definition. The example that follows (figure 5.2) is an adaptation of the Frayer Model, using a graphic organizer.

The targeted word is "raptor." In this fourth grade example, there are a few students who have prior knowledge on the topic. But very often, when

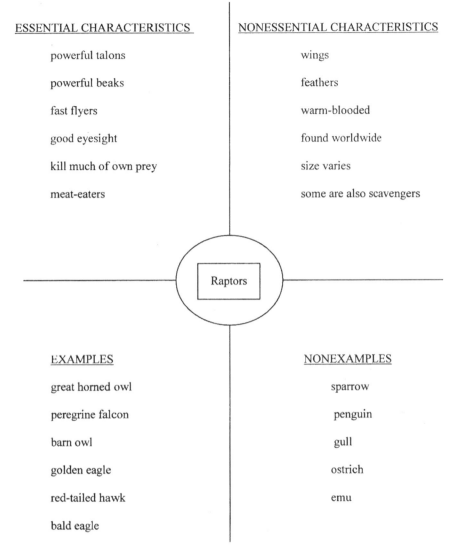

ESSENTIAL CHARACTERISTICS

    powerful talons

    powerful beaks

    fast flyers

    good eyesight

    kill much of own prey

    meat-eaters

NONESSENTIAL CHARACTERISTICS

    wings

    feathers

    warm-blooded

    found worldwide

    size varies

    some are also scavengers

Raptors

EXAMPLES

    great horned owl

    peregrine falcon

    barn owl

    golden eagle

    red-tailed hawk

    bald eagle

NONEXAMPLES

    sparrow

    penguin

    gull

    ostrich

    emu

Figure 5.2. Frayer Model (raptors)

teachers ask children to define a word, the children respond with attributes or defining characteristics anyway: in this case, "Well, it's kind of like a bird, like a hawk or eagle, they eat rabbits and stuff." When asked in this fashion, students do not typically volunteer non-examples and irrelevant properties—but those elements really help to clarify.

An example of a way a Frayer Model can be graphically displayed is shown in figure 5.2.

Semantic Feature Analysis

Semantic Feature Analysis (SFA) (Pittelman, Heimlich, Berglund, & French, 1991) is another relatively time-consuming and labor intensive strategy. It focuses students' attention on the relationship of words within categories. It illustrates how words are both similar and different and emphasizes the uniqueness of each word. Steps in the process include the following:

1. Show students a list of words on the blackboard, SMART Board, or chart paper. The words should share at least one common feature.
2. Have students list some characteristic, quality, or ability possessed by one of the items on the list. Put these words across the top of the board to create a matrix. Then have students fill in the matrix with yes and no, or plus and minus, responses. If items are not completely dichotomous, a number scale can be substituted to suggest the dimmer switch analogy made earlier.
3. When the grid has been completed and discussed, have students expand the matrix by suggesting additional items.

See table 5.1 for an SFA example about birds.

SFA, when done on butcher paper, is more "permanent" than when written on the chalk board—students can then revisit key words more readily. I've

Table 5.1. Semantic Feature Analysis

	Has talons	Has feathers	Has wings	Can fly	Is endangered	Migrates	Is a bird of prey	Is extinct
Blue Jay	−	+	+	+	−	−	−	−
Great Horned Owl	+	+	+	+	−	−	+	−
Roadrunner	-	+	+	−	−	?	+	−
Pelican								
Hummingbird								
Golden Eagle								
Dodo								
Penguin								
Seagull								
Red-Tailed Hawk								

Code: + = yes   − = no   ? = don't know

seen teachers bring the chart paper to the tables where students work, taping it down for students to create this tool as well as the previously mentioned visual organizer. This strategy works well with English language learners.

TEACHING NEW MEANING FOR KNOWN WORDS

Again, these strategies are not mutually exclusive, nor do they fit perfectly. But generally, those that follow are often appropriate for either extending or refining vocabulary when words and concepts are relatively "familiar" to students. Please recall the dimmer switch analogy, and recognize that words are not usually known completely, but that a continuum exists. Remember, too, that any term may be quite familiar to one student in particular, yet virtually unknown to her best friend in the seat next to her.

Students need to realize that common words can at times have technical meanings in the content areas—it is possible, then, for a child to have a pretty sophisticated understanding of a word, only to be confronted with a completely new meaning. Following are some strategies that can help.

Word Analogies

Analogies are wonderful tools for connecting the known to the new, for flexibility and depth in word knowledge, and for overall critical thinking. They certainly work when it comes to connecting vocabulary in narrative text, but they are particularly useful for making connections in the content areas.

Your author sent a manuscript on analogy instruction to the old *Journal of Reading* (now *Journal of Adolescent and Adult Literacy*) in the mid-1980s. One of the reviewers panned the article, saying that analogies were useful for testing vocabulary (as they were utilized customarily at that time) but were not appropriate for *teaching* vocabulary. Since that time we have learned a lot about the interconnecting of instruction and assessment, realizing that at times they should be seamless, mirroring each other—that good formative assessments should look and feel like instruction, that children should not be aware that they are being assessed.

Children need to have vocabulary breadth and depth in order to reason analogically. With proper teacher scaffolding, children as young as second grade can do analogies (Huffbenkoski & Greenwood, 1995). Children need to have explicit instruction in the requisite pieces of analogy instruction, which includes categorization practice, as well as some work with the various types of categories of analogies.

You should work your way back, then, to whole analogies, and use a fill-in-the-blank format as opposed to multiple choice in order to encourage divergent thinking. However, due to high-stakes testing realities, we also owe it to our children to expose them to multiple-choice formats and to instruct them on how to think like a test maker and to arrive at the "one best answer" when necessary, that is, *select* an answer as opposed to constructing one.

MRS. SHAFER'S FOURTH GRADE CLASSROOM

Mrs. Shafer's method of analogy instruction takes place over several days, but is collapsed into the essentials here due to space limitations. She follows a part-whole-part-whole format. Here are the steps:

Mrs. Shafer goes over several multi-meaning words, for example, she writes "switch" on the board and has students pronounce and define the words, making the point that variants of definitions are to be expected without context, when words are in isolation. She also does the same with a word that can have dual pronunciation (e.g., rebel).

Mrs. Shafer then does some easy oral, full (whole) analogies (e.g., grass is to green as snow is _____; April is to spring as January is to _____) and helps the students arrive at a definition of the word "analogy."

She then does a series of grouping and categorizing activities (reminding students that these are not *analogies) where students add one word to a grouping, and then take an item away:*

trumpet, clarinet, oboe, shoe
social studies, baseball, math, science
rectangle, octagon, pentagon, _____
ankle, knee, hip, _____

Mrs. Shafer does a lot of thinking aloud, and has students do the same throughout the process—they must justify their reasoning. As an example, for the last sample grouping activity, they may complete the item with any body part, but they need to recognize that it is more pre-cise to complete it with, say, wrist or elbow because they are joints.

She then engages students in whole analogies, keeping them familiar in terms of vocabulary load. The students work in pairs and do a lot of verbalizing with partners, then with whole class debriefing.

Over time, Mrs. Shafer then eases them into creating analogies made up of social studies and science terms and concepts. She is careful not to incorporate too many unknowns into each analogy. Students engage in solving each others' work.

Following are some student-created analogies, some of which are clearly rooted in social studies and science "content." The possibilities are endless, for they can certainly be applied just as well in foreign language, music, art, mathematics, and general vocabulary areas. Harvey and Goudvis (2006) make a strong case for coding text as an explicit way to teach children to be aware of connections that personalize reading comprehension (e.g., text to text, text to self, text to the world). We discuss, similarly, the personal connections that children make with analogies, with "ah-ha!" realizations as they create novel ways to explore interrelationships among words.

Table 5.2 shows some analogies created by seventh and eighth graders.

Graphic Organizers (Again)

Let's say that the term "lance" is familiar to Sue, a seventh grader, who had an infected blister on her foot lanced by her family doctor a few years prior and (understandably) remembers the incident. However, in reading an Arthurian legend, she comes across the word in the following sentence: "The *page* handed Sir Kay his shield, his sword, and his *lance*. After the knight snapped down his *visor*, the page then handed him his *mace*." Although the word we're focusing on is "lance," let's think about what an unsophisticated reader has to deal with in just this short passage in terms of multi-meaning words.

- *page*: Sue previously knew the word "page" as a part of a book and as someone being called publicly, as at an airport; the meaning of page as a knight's young assistant was new to her prior to reading this story; the teacher pre-taught it with the following analogy—knight : page :: doctor : intern.
- *visor*: She knew visor as part of a hat, to keep the sun out of her face—and the same function on her dad's car—but she wondered about why a knight would want to keep the sun out of his face; Sue studied an illustration of a helmet, and recalled some gladiator movies, and reasoned through what visor meant in the present context.
- *mace*: Her only knowledge of "mace" was the spray that is used in self-defense, the hot peppery stuff with which you defend yourself against a mugger; she doesn't realize it, but from television viewing Sue "knows" what a mace is—she just doesn't know it by that name (she saw *Braveheart* on HBO and had a gruesomely clear understanding of what a mace was).

Table 5.2. Analogies

<table>
<tr><td colspan="2" align="center">Student-Created Analogies</td></tr>
<tr>
<td>

DODGERS : BROOKLYN ::
Lakers : Philadelphia
Falcons : Atlanta
Jazz : Utah
Braves : Milwaukee
</td>
<td>

QUELL : RIOT ::
douse : flame
like : love
calm : fan
abhor : enjoy
</td>
</tr>
<tr>
<td>

STYMIE : IMPEDE ::
ignore : scrutinize
discipline : chasten
decry : praise
exhume : inter
</td>
<td>

ASWAN : NILE ::
Hoover : Colorado
Bagnell : Ozarks
Fort Peck : Montana
Hoover : Nevada
</td>
</tr>
<tr>
<td>

LUMBER : AGILITY
cedar : limberness
cherish : care
timber : speed
offend : tact
</td>
<td>

BROWN : ABOLITIONIST ::
Wright : inventor
Booth : assassin
Whitney : architect
Dickens : essayist
</td>
</tr>
<tr>
<td>

SMOKE SIGNALS : TELEPHONE ::
contacts : glasses
algebra : geometry
antenna : radio
telegraph : satellite
</td>
<td>

LONDON : BUCK ::
Paris : dollar
Hamburg : doe
King : Cujo
Rome : drachma
</td>
</tr>
<tr>
<td>

UNDERTAKER : FUNERAL PARLOR::
trucker : semi
judge : courtroom
electrician : volt meter
teacher : homework
</td>
<td>

ORDINARY : ECCENTRIC ::
predictable : erratic
loyalty : devotee
craven : dastardly
optimistic : positive
</td>
</tr>
<tr>
<td>

CRITICIZE : CASTIGATE ::
adore : like
miniscule : paltry
critic : cast
announce : trumpet
</td>
<td>

LAMB : PEACE ::
elephant : memory
hawk : war
donkey : cunning
rabbit : courage
</td>
</tr>
<tr>
<td>

LEDGER : ACCOUNTANT ::
word processor : secretary
mast : captain
accuser : auditor
chemist : crucible
</td>
<td>

POTTER : WHEEL ::
porter : wagon
cab driver : fare
musician : instrument
computer : word processor
</td>
</tr>
<tr>
<td>

ASPARAGUS : SPEAR ::
carrot : gun
lettuce : green
bass : drum
corn : ear
</td>
<td>

HABIT : NUN ::
helmet : cyclist
baseball : bat
football : punt
priest : bows
</td>
</tr>
</table>

• *lance*: Sue has reasoned that a lance is some type of weapon, and there is even a picture clue—she sees a shield, a sword, a spear, armor, and by process of elimination she decides that (unless the picture cues and the context clues mislead her, which they sometimes do) a lance is another word for a spear—but she's not sure, particularly due to the fact that when she got "lanced" it was just a little needle that was used. So she brings it up for her teacher, and the class constructs a word map (see figure 5.3).

This graphic organizer is a simple, freestyle word map. Hierarchical arrays are also very good ways to organize new and different meanings for otherwise known words.

Typical to Technical Approach

This strategy was outlined by Pearson and Johnson (1984) and enhanced by Welker (1987) and Stahl (1985). Students need to be actively engaged in discussions to clarify the differences between an earlier known definition and a new, enhanced definition, reflecting an expanded meaning. According to Blachowicz and Fisher (2010), the discussion can be time consuming, but

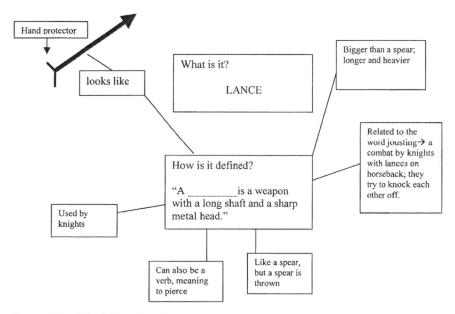

Figure 5.3. Word Map (lance)

the benefits of a rich new understanding "justify the time spent" (p. 87). The three stages of the strategy are as follows:

1. Before introducing the new and technical definition of the targeted word, discuss its common meaning.
2. Have students do word-to-meaning exercises in which they match the words with common definitions and technical definitions. I have enhanced this to include a wrong/inaccurate definition.
3. Develop maze sentences, requiring students to use the targeted word both ways. Again, I've added a sentence that doesn't fit.

   Let's say that the topic is an early introduction to economics, and the fourth graders are getting ready to learn about interest. The "typical" definition, the economics sense of the word, is "a charge for a financial loan, usually a percentage of the amount loaned." After some discussion, the students move to steps 2 and 3.

   Step 2:

Term	*Common Meaning*	*Technical Meaning*	*Wrong Meaning*
interest	fascination	money percentage	happy
firm	hard, solid	company	sad
expire	run out of time	die	doleful

   Step 3:

My mom's charge card has an _____rate of 12 percent.
She has a great _____in horseback riding.
The car sped around the _____.

OPIN

According Vacca and Vacca (2001), this strategy extends meaning vocabulary. OPIN stands for opinion. The class is divided into groups of three, and exercise sentences are distributed to each student. The students complete their sentences individually; then each student must convince the other two in the group that his/her word choice is the best.

   When the groups have trouble reaching consensus, they can take their issue up before the entire class. When all groups have finished, the class discusses the answers. As always, cogent justification is necessary. OPIN encourages differing opinions about which word makes the most sense in a blank space. The roles of prior knowledge and experience are of course critical; additionally, the opportunity for justification of one's answers results in continued attention and active listening. Some sample sentences follow:

Since I was in no hurry, I _____ through the park.
The _____ government of South Africa still rules.
William and my brother are going to _____ in the militia.
Patrick Henry was a famous American _____.
Eli Whitney invented the _____ _____.
Mata Hari was _____ for spying.
Benedict Arnold was guilty of _____.
The Articles of Confederation are a list of _____.

A word box may be used as a scaffold in the beginning.

```
apartheid
patriot
cotton gin
executed
enlist
ambled
treason
parameters
```

Vocabulary-Focused K-W-L

The original K-W-L procedure (Ogle, 1986) is widely used with informational texts. It provides theoretically sound activation of prior knowledge and purpose setting, as students list what they K*now*, W*ant* to know, and (after reading) L*earned* about a topic. A vocabulary-focused K-W-L is appropriate when a selection contains several challenging or critical words. The teacher preselects the key words and guides the students to discuss what they know about the words. Students then develop questions based on the selected vocabulary. The teacher may have them do a variety of activities centered on the words when the reading is finished, from sorting to simply discussing.

The steps in the strategy follow:

1. Select new and/or unfamiliar words.
2. List the words.
3. Lead a discussion of the words students know.

4. Introduce the new meanings for the present topic.
5. Have students generate questions based on the words.
6. Read the text.
7. Ask students to write answers to the questions asked in step 5.
8. Debrief in some fashion: cluster, discuss.

Vocabulary Notebooks

Vocabulary notebooks can be an integral part of students' word learning if they are student driven, and if they are more than repositories for definitions. They can be powerful learning tools if they are treated more like a longitudinal sort of Vocabulary Self-Selection Strategy or bookmark exercise.

Students can take responsibility for the following steps:

1. Mark the text while you are reading, with highlighter or pencil, noting special words to return to.
2. Go back to your marked words; read around the words; think about possible meanings.
3. Write the word, the sentence you found it in, the page number, and an abbreviated title for the text (e.g., *Bless the Beasts and Children* = *BBC*) (teachers need to instruct children in how to use ellipses).
4. Look at different word parts—think about the meaning of the affixes and the root word.
5. Think of other words that are like this one, and write them underneath the part of the word that is similar (optional).
6. Look up the word in the dictionary, read the various definitions, and record the "best fit."
7. Read about the origin of the word, and add it to your entry if you find it interesting (this step is optional).

IT FITS

IT FITS is a mnemonic for a strategy based on keywords (see figure 5.4). It is particularly useful in providing support to struggling readers. The students start with the IT of the mnemonic:

I*dentify* the targeted word.
T*ell* the definition.

The students do this on an index card. Due to previously mentioned shortcomings of dictionaries, lots of guided practice will be necessary in helping strugglers choose the best definition. Anyway, here are the next steps:

F*ind* a keyword you know that will help you to remember the targeted word and write it on the card.

I*magine* a connection.

T*hink* about the connection and draw a picture on the card.

S*tudy* the card until the word is "memorized."

Contextual Redefinition

Naturally occurring context can help, but the teacher can get better mileage out of a "doctored" sentence. Attributed to Tierney, Readence, and Dishner (1985), this is a five-step process that introduces new vocabulary in rich contexts. This works as something walked through whole class and then turned over to groups or individuals. The steps are as follows:

1. *Select unfamiliar words.* As always, select only a few terms that really merit some concentrated instructional time.
2. *Write a rich sentence for each word.* Think about the types of context clues previously presented.
3. *Present the words in isolation.* Use the chalkboard, SMART Board, or a transparency. Guesses may be off base, but have students discuss and come to a consensus.
4. *Now present the words in the sentences.* Then redo the process in step 3, reasoning out a definition. You as teacher need to at first model and think aloud, then delve deeply and elicit students' talk about their thinking.
5. *Dictionary verification.* Designate a person or two to be a verifier/checker. This step provides the opportunity to talk about any interesting word parts, derivations, and so forth.

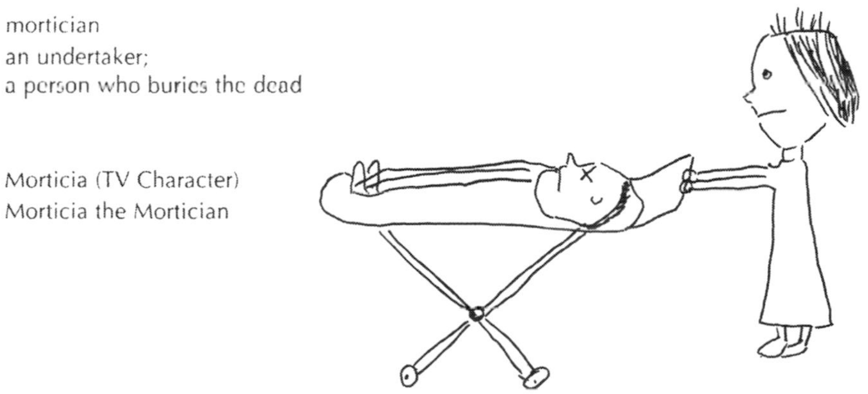

mortician
an undertaker;
a person who buries the dead

Morticia (TV Character)
Morticia the Mortician

Figure 5.4. IT FITS (Morticia)

Here's an example using the word "leukemia":

1. Leukemia
2. Leukemia, a usually fatal disease involving the overproduction of white blood cells, was ruled out.
3. Repeat 1.
4. Repeat 2.
5. Any of a group of usually fatal diseases involving uncontrolled proliferation of leukocytes.

As opposed to common misuses of the dictionary, this is sound use of a valuable tool: to *verify* meanings of new words, often by selecting from among definitions to "match" a given context.

TOAST

TOAST is an acronym that corresponds to the steps in a procedure developed by Dana and Rodriquez (1992) to provide a structure for students to learn vocabulary at their own pace—and to focus on words that present the most challenge. TOAST involves the students in the following steps:

T*est*. Students pretest themselves, or with a partner, orally or in written form. In this first step, they ascertain which words are already known versus partially known versus unknown. The authors suggest making vocabulary cards for the words to be learned.
O*rganize*. Students then organize their words into some kind of framework, according to familiarity or semantic relation.
A*nchor*. Students have a number of "rehearsal" options: reciting to a partner; using a tape recorder; finding an original mnemonic link. The object is to get the words into long term memory.
S*ay*. This is the review stage. Depending on the child, vocabulary needs to be relearned as necessary.
T*est*. This should be student conducted!

TOAST is a bit formulaic, but it has its merits, particularly for struggling readers and second language learners. It can offer a viable combination of structure *and* student control.

The Intelligent Guess Strategy

This strategy is used as either a pre-reading or a post-reading tool. But either way it requires students to think about words, and to focus on how the context

Table 5.3. Intelligent Guess

Vocabulary Word	Intelligent Guess	Clues to Help Make Guess	Dictionary Entry	Original Sentences
gelding				
fetlocks				
paddock				
scalpel				
groom				

influences meaning. It's another way to integrate dictionary use, and students must think deeply about grammar and subtle clues.

Have students divide a page into five columns. The columns are done in installments: the first three are one cluster; the last two columns can be completed at the end of the unit. The five columns are word, intelligent guess, clues to help make guess, dictionary entry, and original sentences. The teacher picks the words, but this process can be turned over to the students after some modeling.

The headers are self-explanatory. Like several of the other strategies, the requirement that the students have to figure out the dictionary meaning that best fits the particular context is a real key. Table 5.3 gives an example of what an intelligent guess matrix will look like.

The key, as always, is discussion and explication. A good teacher can cajole/demand/require that students be sure to write original sentences that are rich and explicit enough so that unknown others can figure out, pretty precisely, what the targeted word means. "I saw the scalpel" just is not acceptable. "The surgeon used the scalpel to cut a three-inch incision in the horse's abdomen" provides so much more information about the students' knowledge.

Please consider the possibilities of layering in these strategies—but you must know your own thresholds and build your students' capacities incrementally! It is time for content area teachers to demystify word learning.

Chapter Six

Vocabulary and Writing

I can't write five words but that I change seven.

—Dorothy Parker

LAST DAY OF SCHOOL

A fifth grade teacher took over a class for the second semester of the academic year. She bonded well with the children, and the last day was a mixture of tears and cartwheels of glee. As the students were walking out for the last time, getting ready for summer vacation, one young man gave a hug and said, "Thanks a lot. I learned a lot." Seconds later, he popped his head back in the door and said he'd been puzzled by one thing. He said, "What does 'vagoo' [rhymes with Magoo] mean?" The teacher was puzzled. He walked back in the room and wrote on the chalk board V-A-G-U-E! He said, "You wrote it on my papers about ten times this year!"

Teachers constantly run into a "problem" when they're about to start a core novel or a read aloud, and a number of students whine, "I already read that!" Ralph Fletcher says to say, "Good, now we'll read like a writer" (Fletcher, 1996). Gary Paulsen says, "Read like a wolf eats." (Paulson, 1993)." Ravenous readers develop large vocabularies that stand them in good stead as listeners, speakers, readers, and writers. This chapter will focus on *writing* vocabulary, but I remind you that we can only artificially separate writing and reading.

Three of the commonly accepted "different" vocabularies are a reading vocabulary, a writing vocabulary, and a speaking vocabulary. There is also a listening vocabulary, meaning words that are understood, but not, unfortunately, *used* by the recipient. Finally there is also a writer's secret vocabulary. About fifteen years ago a friend saw a book on oxymorons. It was replete with many clever illustrations, and she became very conversant with what oxymorons were. The problem was, she had never heard anyone *use* the word orally and was afraid to pronounce it. So she kept it tucked away in her "secret vocabulary" until she was comfortable enough to unveil it.

A strong vocabulary provides the writer with the tools to get a richness of thought onto the paper. However, the real artistry of the writer comes not from using an esoteric, impressive word—it comes from using the *right* word the *right* way. Ernest Hemingway, for example, was known for his economical word choice. Teachers need to share with their students the pleasure in finding the exact word that conveys a particular nuance.

An author's selection of words brings persons, plus objects, and feelings to life in the "eyes" of the reader. Words are selected carefully in order to influence the reader to believe or do something. Again, please note how figure 6.1 gives detail to figure 3.1.

THE THESAURUS

A thesaurus is essentially a book of synonyms that can help to narrow the search for that perfect word. The name "Roget" is inextricably connected to the word "thesaurus." To coin an analogy, dictionary: Webster :: thesaurus : Roget.

Roget attempted to organize and classify all human knowledge. His monumental undertaking evolved into sections of the first Roget's thesaurus (1852). Using his thesaurus was difficult, for it was organized by theme, not in alphabetical order. Another difficulty is the very notion of what constitutes an "exact" synonym. For a purist, no two words are precisely synonyms—but they certainly can be close. Synonyms, then, are words with similar meanings.

Most modern thesauri are, of course, alphabetically organized, and for each key word are synonyms, definitions, and (often) antonyms. The thesaurus is an important tool for professional writers, and should be so as well for all writers, no matter what their level of expertise. It should be noted that there are thesauri out there for young children as well as older students.

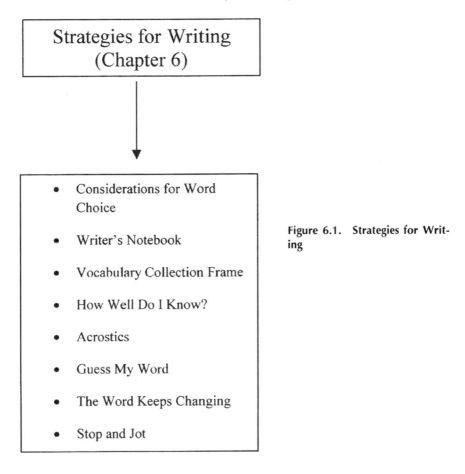

Figure 6.1. Strategies for Writing

REVISION: THE PROCESS

The word "revision" literally means to see again. And although the process of writing may be on the wane due to current emphasis on product, the best minds in the field are nearly unanimous in this area—despite some variety of opinion elsewhere—what is critical to all writers is the necessity for revision. Going back to the writer's purpose, it's clear that in order to communicate effectively, writers need to practice the art of "re-visioning" as many times as necessary in order to "get it right." Put bluntly, the proponents of the writing process have been losing the battle to those who, philosophically, have more invested in the bottom line: product.

According to Spandel and Stiggins (1997), "revision is that part of the writing process that truly allows a writer to see again" to "re-vision what she has written" (p. 102). In short, we teach students to think. The art and craft of revision is very difficult to teach. Barry Lane has written a very useful book called *After the End*. He found that students wrote THE END at "the end" of each draft and rarely revised their work. "Even teachers . . . viewed revision as simply making a 'sloppy copy' picture—perfect instead of as a means of discovery. Nothing new came after 'THE END'" (Lane, 1993, p. 2). Following are some reminders:

- Remember the importance of the prewriting stage of the process—webbing and sketching help young writers to organize and outline their thoughts.
- Remember the power of rich oral language and wide reading—writers have to be readers! If a "just right" word is not in the mental lexicon, then it's not going to be available to be recalled!
- Remember the importance of risk taking and safety for your students—praise and encourage children who stretch themselves—reward these efforts, and refrain from red inking.
- Remember to model and encourage active seeking of "just right" words during all phases of the process (whatever process fits) but *especially as they revise*.
- Remember flexibility and fluency in writing vocabulary use—provide plenty of student choice, but don't abdicate your responsibilities as teacher.

Johnson and Pearson (1978) discuss their three Rs: reducing, rearranging, and rewording. Reducing means eliminating, rearranging means moving around, and rewording means selective changing of key words. All involve more effective communication, with attention to word choice, detail, and figurative language.

I remember, when in sixth grade long ago, my teacher requiring everyone to turn in an outline with a research paper. The formal type of outline that was in vogue at the time baffled me:

I.
    A.
    B.
II.
    A.
    B.
        1.
        2.
        3.
            a.
            b.
            c.

What I did was write the paper, then develop an outline that matched after the fact.

Writing aficionados who are conversant with "the writing process" understand more and more that it's all about helping writers to develop *their* process rather than to follow "the" five-step process in lockstep. What truly is critical for all writers, novice to published, is the necessity for revision. James Michener once said, "I'm not a very good writer, but I'm an excellent rewriter." There are very few writers so gifted that they can get it right the first time. Whatever approach writing teachers use, revision is essential, for it helps writers polish and improve their piece.

BROAD REMINDERS

For vocabulary and writing connections, we need to remember Blachowicz and Fisher (2010) and their analogy of the dimmer switch vis-à-vis the on/off switch. That's a true foundation of this book: word knowledge is not an all-or-nothing proposition. Words are known at different levels. Beck, McCaslin, and McKeown (1980) termed their levels of word knowledge as *unknown*, *acquainted*, and *established*, although there are levels in between (e.g., when you ask your children about a word and they say "I've heard of it" but that's all that's there). There's a level between unknown and acquainted, and . . . what the heck, let's create our own continuum, starting with the categories of Beck and colleagues, and building from there (see figure 6.2).

Now here's the distinction that must be made. For *listening* purposes, realistically, most of the language children hear is very basic. And honestly, unless they're very curious and assertive, occasional words can be uttered that are unknown, and the purpose of the conversation isn't lost. A sixth grade teacher asked a question, got an answer, and said that the proffered answer was "plausible." The students immediately asked her what "plausible" meant,

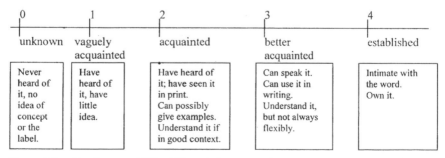

Figure 6.2.   Continuum of Word Knowledge

and that was addressed easily enough, for it was only a new term/label for an easily understood concept. The teacher and the class talked about what would be a plausible reason for being an hour late, coming home after curfew on a Friday night. Being kidnapped by aliens and being held hostage would not be plausible: the battery on your watch wearing out would qualify as being plausible, if not totally acceptable.

In the preceding situation, the teacher took advantage of a teachable moment in oral discourse. Another factor in learning words aurally is that, as opposed to print, the speaker can either be interrupted and explicitly *asked* questions, or can "read" the body language of listeners (nodded assent, or quizzical tilt of the head) and clarify meaning. This does not happen with other mediums of communication. So, listening (depending on who the speaker is) can result in strengthened vocabulary, but words can be presented at the low end of the continuum without too much harm.

Depending on text and context, as the case was made earlier, students can still be comprehending when confronted with a certain number of words at the zero and one levels on our newly printed continuum (figure 6.2). Remember that "natural" context only results in about a 5 percent chance of retention/learning/knowing per exposure. But if we can move some words in our "one" category over to "two" and "three" through a combination of wide reading and targeted instruction, it will serve children well.

Now, here's the crux of this chapter—after all, the focus is *writing* and vocabulary connectivity. When a child hears and/or reads new and challenging words, there can and will be a number of ones and twos (remember the continuum from Beck and her colleagues), and few "zero" (unknown) words—but they can be tolerated and dealt with, and they are ephemeral, in that they float in the air or waft through the mind, and they "disappear." But for a young person to *write* a word for authentic communicative purposes, it had better be in at least the three category on our continuum.

In writing, fortunately, there is more time to really deal with "just right" words. Children and adults can be impetuous, but we need to be clear about the necessity for them to use both the *time* and *resources* available in order to get the word "right" and to *get the right word*. Written words are not ephemeral; they are captured in time and space, and stand as monuments to their author's communicative competence.

(Parenthetically, when researchers estimate the number [around three thousand] of new words a child "learns" in a year, one cannot help but wonder how they define "learning." They are probably not talking about flexible, deep, thorough ownership. It is most likely a more basic understanding of words and their derivations.)

Janet Allen (2007) contends that words must be taught at different levels depending on their importance, frequency, and applicability in other contexts. When students can generate good uses of words in their writing, they are at least at our three level, possibly a four. Finally, when children (and adults) use words in their own *oral language*, they most probably do "own" them and have their meanings "nailed." Again depending on audience and purpose, they'll typically use only a small percentage of words they know/recognize in the speech or writing they produce. Remember, one does not value her own word knowledge for the purpose of impressing her friends. Rather, there are two major purposes: to increase her reading comprehension and to improve the range and specificity of her writing. We then must convey the same thing to our students.

CLICHÉS

I was teaching a lesson on metaphors and similes to my seventh graders. We overlapped that with clichés; the children thought some of the old clichés were a real hoot. We talked about painting pictures with words, so that our readers could truly "see" the image(s) intended. We ticked off a number of the hackneyed clichés.

- *as cold as ice*
- *as pretty as a picture*
- *as neat as a pin*
- *as quick as a wink*

The students stopped and conjectured about the origins of some— they wondered, for example, how a pin could exemplify neatness. Then I had them work on new and different comparisons:

- *as cold as a gambler's glare*
- *as hot as Tim Duncan in a zone*

Those in the classroom love the work of Ralph Fletcher, who reminds us of the power and wonder of words—they are the paints in the author's palette that enable him or her to communicate fully and richly with the reader.

Written words are monuments that are captured and frozen and are open to scrutiny and revisitation. Spoken words are rather temporary—the reader can err, misunderstand, and often nobody knows or cares. When students are readers, they need to recognize words and assign meaning to them. When they are speaking, depending upon their purpose and audience, they quickly choose words that hopefully get their message across—but if they don't find the best word, it disappears and is forgotten. But when one writes, she must really deliberate (and sometimes agonize) over choices.

A writer has an *obligation* to select the right words for her intended audience. In addition to the obligation, there is a certain amount of pressure the writer puts on herself. Reading, speaking, and writing are all communication processes—but writing is by far the most exacting, the most laborious, the most painful. Red Smith once said, "Writing is easy. All you have to do is sit down at a typewriter and open a vein."

WORD CHOICE FOR WRITING

Process writing methodologies have changed the landscape of the teaching of writing. It used to be that writing was assigned and corrected, but rarely was it actually *taught*. Although the stages of the writing process are somewhat fluid, three broad stages are usually identified: planning, creating, and reviewing. Word selection comes into play during all three stages. According to Flower and Hayes (1994),

> [A]s composing proceeds, a new element enters the task environment which places even more constraints upon what the writer can say. Just as a title constrains the content of a paper and topic sentence shapes the options of the paragraph, each word in the growing text determines and limits the choices of what comes next. (p. 934)

Keys to good word choice are the writer's sense of purpose and sense of audience. Unless one is engaged in self-reflective writing (e.g., a diary; when, as another example, one writes a grocery list, it doesn't matter whether cantaloupe is misspelled), one always writes for a purpose, with a certain audience in mind. In my estimation, the most deadly and limiting "audience" is the teacher. Writing only for the teacher leads to uninspired writing. For meaningful writing to occur, a real plus is a lively, authentic audience to write for.

CONSIDERATIONS FOR WORD CHOICE

The following are adapted from Johnson (2001). They relate to words needing to be precise, so that the writer can make the optimal word choice. These considerations are the following:

Abstract—Concrete

Abstract words connote ideas that cannot be directly experienced (e.g., truth, beauty, love, jealousy) whereas concrete words (e.g., Philadelphia Phillies baseball cap, the Comcast Center, a fourteen-foot python) can be seen, touched, and directly experienced. A good writer mixes and matches abstract and concrete words, *and* helps her reader make sense of these words through analogies and examples. Remember, too, that most words are not either abstract or concrete, rather, they exist along a continuum:

machine   vehicle   automobile   SUV   2003 Ford Explorer

Specific—General

Specific words name the members of the class, which is named by the general word. Johnson (2001) states that general words are called hypernyms, whereas specific words are hyponyms. These are often represented in graphic organizers (see figure 6.3).

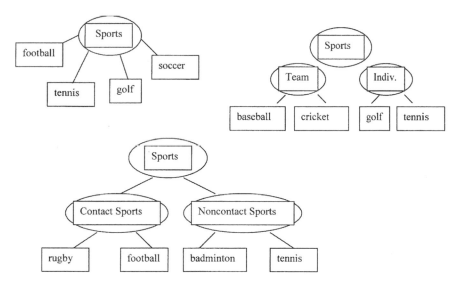

Figure 6.3.   Specific to General Word Maps

Ambiguous—Explicit

We are well aware of the fact that we have many multi-meaning words in our language. That's a given. But *ambiguous* words are unclear even in context—because of bad/careless/imprecise context. Some examples:

I cannot recommend this person too highly.
You will be lucky to get this person to work for you.
Robert put on quite a performance.

Writers need to be aware of potential ambiguities, and of course can make words more explicit with careful contextualizing.

All good writers must then find a way to choose the right word that gets the message across clearly. Usually the perfect word is right there in the writer's mental lexicon, but sometimes a thesaurus is called for. The writer also needs to take care that any potential ambiguities are addressed via rich, explicit context.

When young writers "conference," they at times are reluctant to make changes, for fear that the process will never end. Additionally, slavish adherence to too many process steps can produce writers who spend enormous amounts of time for very small output and have trouble shifting among different kinds of writing. Students are ill served by the exclusivity that unfortunately has framed the sometimes overly linear aspects of an otherwise good idea.

USING THE WRITER'S NOTEBOOK

Teachers can use the writer's notebook for multiple purposes. It can be thought of like a sketchpad, and we see it as a flexible tool for all writers, young and old. It also is akin to a haven, an incubator, where seeds of writing can grow, or flourish, or languish, or be plowed under. Typical musts are for the writer's notebook to contain a dialogue journal and a "word collection" section, as well as miscellaneous lists of quotes, pictures, and so forth.

As a form of Vocabulary Self-Selection (see chapter 4), you may have students keep a personal vocabulary section of their writer's notebook, with the intent to *use* many of these words in pieces future and present. Have the children further divide the section into formal and informal parts. The formal part is pretty structured (as will be related shortly), but the informal words need only be listed (and identified as to their source/origin) and eventually categorized. Both groupings are very personal and unique.

Jason, a sixth grader, selected fifteen words from his Sustained Silent Reading book:

debonair	subtly	deafening
exasperation	bowled	surrogate
belligerently	piercingly	slyly
tickle	indignantly	careened
angora	assurance	arrogant

He just let the list lie dormant for a while; when he was done with the book, he wanted to go back to five of the words for in-depth study and incorporation into his writing.

Danielle, on the other hand, negotiated as part of her learning contract to go into depth with all fifteen of her self-selected words.

eccentric	lack	arson
spay	solemnly	anxiety
quizzical	cunning	marathon
intimidated	colleagues	descende
admiration	scowling	waggled

Each word was written down in at least partial context, and an appropriate definition was selected for each; for example, "eccentric":

"The *eccentric* inventor is driving cross-country."
very unusual or odd; not normal; literally "off center"

With other children, words should periodically be shared, traded, and enjoyed. They can be sorted, played with, or just plain admired. When students are working on a unit of study or in a writing workshop, the vocabulary notebook serves as both a resource and a place to collect words. The writer's notebook can, of course, be tailored to meet more developmentally advanced needs. As an example, students can "collect" interesting words from lyrics of their favorite songs (years ago a sixth grader "banked" the word "maniacal" from Michael Jackson's *Thriller*). More recently a student picked "shibboleth" from Shawn Colvin and "diffident" from the Gin Blossoms. Without "forcing" new words, try to incorporate them in their writing if they are, indeed, "just right" words.

Students should also be encouraged to use their writer's notebooks to find and collect interesting quotes and juxtapositions:

"Time wounds all heels."
"It's not the men in my life, it's the life in my men."
Ponderings/imponderables: "If cats like to eat mice so much, why don't they make mouse-flavored cat food?"

More examples are coming up in chapter 9 and in the appendices.

SPECIFIC STRATEGIES

What *do* we do? Many of the strategies for word learning in chapters 4 and 5 are excellent for reading or writing vocabulary. Here are a few more strategies that are particularly good for writing vocabulary.

Vocabulary Collection Frame

The frame shown in figure 6.4 is adapted from Wood (2001).

How Well Do I Know?

This is also a good assessment, serving as an aid to the teacher in deciding which words to pre-teach (see figure 6.5).

Acrostics

For younger children in particular, acrostics offer endless possibilities for using words imaginatively and descriptively. They can promote risk taking because they typically do not require words to be used in formal context. Because there are fewer words to deal with than in a longer story or other genres, students really focus on the new words that must be the right words. See the example that follows.

Vocabulary Collection

My new word is _____.

I found it_____.

The reason I chose it is _____.

The context was_____.

I think it means_____.

My original sentence is

_____

_____.

Figure 6.4.   Vocabulary Collection Frame

How Well Do I Know

Title/Source:_____

Check out the words listed below. Prior to reading, these are words that I <u>think</u> we should go over.

Know It Well	Think I Know It	Clueless	During Reading: My Choices

Words:

Figure 6.5. How Well Do I Know

*B*ouncing the rock
w*A*iting
a*S*
fol*K*s
*E*dge forward in
*T*heir seats . . .
*B*am!
*A*nd I
g*L*ide in for a
*L*ayup!

Acrostics afford children the opportunity to reflect upon complex ideas and important vocabulary in their content area subjects. They are a way for your students to delight others and convey their learning using something other than an expository (usually dry!) form of writing.

Acrostics can report science facts and information in a personal form. Again, focus is on using the "just right" vocabulary. In mathematics, the specialized language of numbers is connected to words. Whatever the topic, do group flexibly.

Guess My Word

This is a simple activity to get children to open up and share orally. Here's an example:

Words that start with T:

- The _____ beat the hare.
- After paying his fare, he walked through the _____ and got on the subway.
- An elephant's snout is called its _____.
- We transport goods from place to place in a _____.

Words that start with L:

- The words of a song are called its _____.
- The slogan of a company is on its _____.
- When we coat something in plastic we _____ it.
- A cowboy's rope is called a _____.

The Word Keeps Changing

This is a great activity for sharing and learning new words.

- I couldn't believe how _____the water was.
  - begins with r
  - begins with m
  - begins with c
  - begins with w
- All in all, it was a _____day.
  - begins with f
  - begins with t
  - begins with w
  - begins with e

Stop and Jot

This is a very flexible "writing-to-learn" strategy that can be applied a number of different ways. It can be done whole class, small group, or one on one.

Start off doing it during read aloud. At a designated spot in the reading, stop and jot down (on a Post-it) a question or a prediction. Then transcribe it onto chart paper, talk about jotting, then read on. Then have the students stop and jot. At the end of each lesson they can transcribe what's on their Post-it, or simply accumulate them.

You can also use stop and jot for vocabulary. At designated points in read alouds, during silent reading of core texts, or during self-selected reading, have the students stop and jot a word that's new or interesting. And, germane to this chapter, sometimes have them choose words that they intend to incorporate into their writing. Remember that to stop and jot means to do so quickly, so they can get back to the act of reading.

TROUBLE SHOOTING

Make sure that vocabulary learning is rooted in wide reading, then polished during the revision stage of some form of process writing. When problems occur, here are some troubleshooting techniques to use when the students are engaged in process writing:

Word Choice Problems: Vocabulary Too Simple

Read aloud any piece that is richly expressive, such as excerpts from Garrison Keillor, possibly Jerry Spinelli, or Gary Paulson. As the students listen, have them actively stop and jot their favorite expressions. Then have them share their choices, and talk about why they are favorites. What words really create mental pictures?

Also brainstorm lists of "tired," worn-out words—and then discuss their alternatives. For example, "nice" and "good" and "bad" (in the case of "bad," for example, kids will go to the thesaurus to find a range of synonyms from "awful" to "naughty" to "horrendous" to "horrific" to "terrible" to "inclement" to "misbehaving" to "spoiled"). But don't stop there, have the children consider connotation while doing simple sorting or semantic gradients (chapter 5). They might group the bad family under describing *food*, describing *weather*, or describing *behavior*. "Bad" behavior might be "naughty" or "disobedient" but we wouldn't use those adjectives to describe either food or the weather. Involve students in the creation of word wheels, posters, or other environmental print that ensures easy access at the time that they choose to revisit words.

Word-of-the-day calendars are also viable tools. Best would be to purchase a commercial one, but use it actively—*and* have students "match" it with daily words of their own. Rather than peel off the pages and discard them, discuss the words, their nuances, and the probability of ever using them in their future writings. Give these words, commercial and matched, critical reviews. Decide what genre to use them in, discuss what audiences would appreciate and relate to them. Think: is there a more accessible word that would do the job better? A colleague hates the word "utilize" being, ahem, utilized, when the simpler word "use" will suffice. Save the daily words, bind them, laminate them, make them convenient for children to revisit.

Word Choice Problems: Overwriting

Try to find some authentic pieces that are overwritten, that is, filled with clichés, long words, or otherwise difficult to understand. If necessary, embellish them even more, to make them *really* unwieldy. Then have the students make them lean and mean—absolutely free of clichés, jargon, and extraneous "fluff."

As a challenge, have the students (you can try group writing for this one) write a piece using only one-syllable words.

Or have the students look up a word in the thesaurus. Use the word in a meaningful sentence. Then try substituting some alternative offered by the thesaurus.

Word Choice Problems: Vocabulary-Audience Match

Give students a passage from a text for which the audience is fairly clearly defined; for example,

1. a music magazine for teens;
2. directions for safety for the early elementary grades (e.g., CPR).

Then ask the students to rewrite the passages for a completely different audience.

1. Adapt the music magazine's message for middle aged adults.
2. Adapt the safety directions for a teenage audience.

Then spend some time having students create their own topics for specialized audiences. Have them talk about their word choice and how to match it to the intended audience.

SOME FINAL FUN ACTIVITIES

As this chapter winds up, here are a few more fun things to try with your students to encourage vocabulary growth, particularly expanding written vocabulary. All of these need to be modeled and talked about if you expect them to "stick."

Eliminate Words

Teach your students how to be more economical, particularly in cases such as these. Some words are unnecessary and redundant.

* In my *personal* opinion, Pete Rose should be in the Hall of Fame.
* Joe Friday was only interested in the *true* facts.
* The film began at 10 a.m. *in the morning.*

Synonym Game

Shift a letter (just one!) from one word to the other in the pair to form synonyms:

Example: simulate and spurt: take the t from spurt to create stimulate and spur

trough	study
bawl	fright
sick	trod
contract	each

The need for written fluency and clarity must not become lost in the standards-crazed shuffle! Words must be learned well in order to become part of a middle level student's bank. You and your children need permission to enjoy yourselves a bit as you work with words.

Chapter Seven

Structural Analysis and Word Parts

Only the educated are free.

—Epictetus, First Century

CHIVVY

Western Pennsylvania, small rural district, my first teaching job. In addition to five sections of tenth grade English, I am awarded an eighth grade "corrective" reading class. I am fresh out of college, and have always been a good reader. Some of these young people are really struggling. The first week of class, with the eighth graders, I am making a point about silent letters—the students are reading a story, and the word "beret" is mispronounced—the reader says "berette." I try to seize this teachable moment. I talk a bit about silent letters, then write the word "Chevrolet" on the board to illustrate his point. When I ask for a volunteer to pronounce the word and give its meaning, Jim Floyd raises his hand. I say, "What's the word?" Jim responds, "Chivvy."

Now at this time I had heard BMWs called "beamers," and Corvettes called "vettes," but I'm doggedly sticking to my impromptu plan and I want the word—Chevrolet, dagnabbit—to be identified so that I can make my point. So I try again with Jim Floyd. I ask again, "What's the word?" Again, the reply: "Chivvy." I then try breaking the word apart, attacking it patiently, covering up parts. To Jim it's just "Chivvy." Jim, it turns out, works at the service station his father owns. He can tune a Chivvy, rebuild a Chivvy engine, do any number of things that I cannot. But Jim is a virtual nonreader with a storehouse of sight words that are

his minimal words, among them, Chivvy. Jim has a small storehouse of
words memorized and readily available. If he doesn't know a word by
sight, he's without a clue.

All literate individuals use their knowledge of word parts to help unlock
the meaning—and often to confirm the meaning—of unfamiliar words. This
use of *structural analysis*, coupled with contextual information, narrows the
possibilities and aids in making meaning. This is often done by analogy with
known words, connecting to the new. As an example, if a student recognizes
that a paraprofessional is a not fully certified assistant teacher, she can infer
that a paramedic is a trained but not fully certified medic. Similarly, paralegal
makes sense, but how about "parachute?" Structural analysis is not foolproof
as a methodology, but it can certainly be helpful in figuring out new words.

Although many roots are learned by repetition and analogy, some readers
were taught them in school—particularly the high utility ones, and the Latin
and Greek roots. Unlike Jim Floyd and his limitation to whole word strategies, most readers learn many new words by taking them apart. This is much
more sophisticated an undertaking than the ubiquitous admonition to "sound
it out." As the chapter unfolds, you will again be asked to return to certain
key figures to see the big picture. They are categorized as "general" word-
learning tools because they are useful across a broad spectrum.

SOME BASICS

Morphemes

A morpheme is the smallest unit of meaning in a language. For example, "dressing" has two morphemes: dress and ing. Although words may have several morphemes, there is a general distinction between *free* morphemes, which can stand
alone, and *bound* morphemes, which need to be attached to another morpheme.
So, as an example, in the word "undressed," un- and -ed are bound morphemes
and "dress" is a free morpheme. We call free morphemes *root* words, recognizing that two roots (e.g., basketball) can be joined together to make compound
words. Bound morphemes are prefixes and suffixes. We will address roots, prefixes, suffixes, and compound words. The jury is out regarding the best way to
teach these "pieces" of language. Let's start with compound words.

Compound Words

Remember, the purview of this book is grades 4–9. A great way to begin
structural analysis work is with compound words. Students instinctively and

naturally break the word into both component parts, because both carry meaning. Simply have the children brainstorm compound words that they know.
Here is part of a list done by fourth graders:

playpen	doghouse	madhouse
underdog	boyfriend	waterfall
football	girlfriend	broadcast
basketball	spoilsport	teenager

Work with students on the "literal" type of compounds, for example, "girlfriend," and the idiomatic or figurative types, for example, "underdog." It's also interesting to note that words like "doghouse" may be used literally or figuratively. The teacher should confront the issues of hyphenated words and words that go together like "open house" but are not joined. We also keep lists of words that are made up of two "words," like "friendless," that are not compound words. Unsophisticated children will say, for example, that "friend" and "ship" are both words; therefore "friendship" is a compound word. It's not that simple. The rules for hyphenations have never been totally clear, either. It seems to me that some words that are now compounds used to be hyphenated, for example, "junk-yard" became "junkyard."

Incidental Structural Analysis Teaching

As opposed to explicitly starting with lists of words or lists of word parts, Manzo and Manzo (1990) advocate taking advantage of teachable moments by only teaching structural analysis in context. What this philosophy lacks in systematicity, it makes up for in salience and meaning. Once the word appears in print, it is presented with useful parts underlined: <u>mono</u>cle. The students are then asked to define the word, if possible. The teacher then gives level 1 and, if necessary, level 2 clues. The level 1 clues are essentially analogy, and are rather subtle—the level 2 clues leave little doubt.

	mono	*cle*
Level 1	monotone	ocular
	monopoly	binocular
Level 2	one	having to do with vision, sight
Definition	An instrument, like glasses, that only corrects vision in one eye.	
Example	"Mr. Peanut" of Planter's Peanuts is known are recognized for his top hat and his monocle.	

	sub	*terranian*
Level 1	submarine	terrain
	substandard	terrafirma
Level 2	under	ground
Definition	underground (literally)	
Example	The Morlocks were subterranian creatures in the early science fiction classic *The Time Machine*, written by H. G. Wells (1988).	

It's a bit of an oxymoron, but this is very explicit incidental learning. The use of context supports the learning of the word, and in the best of worlds students will have some elements of this presentation overlapped with targeted word part lists. Finally, see to it that the students internalize the level 1 and level 2 clues, and the best way to do *that* is to self-select the words and develop their own clues.

HIGH UTILITY STRUCTURES AND STRATEGIES

Root Words and Word Parts

According to various researchers, teaching young adolescents about ninety high utility Greek and Latin word parts is a good expenditure of time and effort. On average late-elementary school students' vocabulary includes about 10 percent of these words. Roots such as "port," meaning "to carry," or "trans," meaning "to send," would certainly qualify as high utility and worth teaching. The learning of roots beyond those (approximately) ninety would not be a good idea due to time-cost factors.

Roots are most likely to stick when taught in word families (as an example, "aud" means "to hear," the family being audition, auditorium, audible, audience, audiovisual, and the like). Here are some high-frequency Greek (G) and Latin (L) roots and word parts:

Root/Parts	*Meaning*	*Examples*
aero (G)	air	aerobics, aerodynamics, aeronautics
agri (L)	field	agriculture, agrarian, agronomy
alt (L)	high	altitude, alto, exalt
ambul (L)	walk	ambulance, amble, somnambulent
andr (G)	man	androgynous, android
belli (L)	war	belligerent, bellicose, rebellion
biblio (G)	book	bibliography, bible
cap (L)	head	caption, capital, decapitate

cardi (G)	heart	cardiologist, cardiac, cardiogram
centr (L)	center	eccentric, egocentric, centrifugal
chron (G)	time	chronological, anachronism
cline (L)	to lean	incline, decline, disinclination
cred (L)	believe	credit, incredible, incredulous
cycl (G)	circle, ring	bicycle, tricycle, cycle, cyclone
dent (L)	tooth	dentist, trident, indent
duc (L)	lead	duct, induct, conduct
fac (L)	do, make	manufacture, facsimile
fid (L)	faith	fidelity, infidelity, confidence, infidel
flex (L)	bend	reflex, flexible, flexor
funct (G)	perform	function, malfunction, dysfunctional
gen (G)	birth, race	generate, genocide, progeny
graph (G)	write	autograph, telegraph, phonograph
homo (L)	man	homicide, homage, hombre
hydr (G)	water	hydrant, dehydrated, hydrogen, hydrophobia
init (L)	beginning	initiate, initiative, initial
ject (L)	throw	project, inject, trajectory
laps (L)	slip	elapse, collapse, relapse
loc (L)	place	locate, location, dislocate, relocate
lust (L)	shine	luster, lackluster, illustrious, illustration
man (L)	hand	manacle, manual, manuscript
mania (G)	madness	maniac, maniacal, pyromania, kleptomania
migr (L)	change, move	migrate, immigrate, migratory, emigrate
morph (G)	shape	amorphous, polymorphous, morphology
mort (L)	death	mortal, immortal, mortgage
neg (L)	no	negative, renege, renegade, negate
numer (L)	number	numeral, numerous, enumerate
nym (G)	name	pseudonym, homonym, synonym, acronym
ortho (G)	straight, right	orthodox, orthodontist, orthopedics, unorthodox
ped/pod (L)	foot	pedal, pedestrian, podiatrist, gastropod
phil (G)	love	philosophy, philanthropy, Philadelphia, philanthropist
poly (L)	many	polygamy, monopoly, polyunsaturated, polyester
port (L)	carry	portage, import, transport, export, deport

psych (G)	mind, soul	psyche, psychology, psychopath, psychiatrist
quest (L)	ask, seek	request, inquest, quest
rupt (L)	break	interrupt, rupture, erupt
san (L)	health	sanitary, insane, sanguine
soph (G)	wise	sophisticated, philosopher
stas, stat (L)	rest, at rest	statue, static, statistic, statute
struct (L)	build	construct, construction, structure, destruct
therm (G)	heat	thermometer, thermal, thermostat
trib (L)	give	contribute, attribute, distribute
urb (L)	city	urban, urbane, suburb
vac (L)	empty	vacate, vacuum, vacation, vacuous
vict (L)	conquer	victory, victim, conviction, convict
voc (L)	voice	convocation, invoke, vocal, vociferous

Affixes

Knowledge of common prefixes and suffixes is very useful in generating meanings of new words. Due to the fact that many words with common affixes (rerun, preseason, unhappy) occur in most children's speaking and listening vocabularies, instruction can begin with what children already know, and then move to the unknown.

Prefixes

Prefixes tend to be more reliable for teaching purposes than suffixes. Many of them are consistent in meaning and spelling. According to Harris and Sipay (1990), four prefixes (un-, re-, in-, and dis-) account for about half of the common prefixed words in English, and twenty prefixes account for all (nearly) prefixed words. There are various schools of thought regarding teaching of prefixes. Some experts use a context and definition procedure very systematically, whereas others recommend a less linear approach. A four-step adaptation follows.

1. Explain the prefix, for example, dis-.
2. With the students, construct a word family list (for example—disinterested, displeased, displace, disrespect, disenchanted, disarm, disincentive, discomfort, disobey). Then discuss the meanings of the words.
3. Try making up some logical, but not actual words:
   disportable = stationary

dismission = not allowed
disopponent = friend
dismania = sanity
disgamy = divorce
disdental = toothless

4. Have your students create their own "new" words and illustrate them. This step should be taken sparingly, if at all, due again to time-cost factors. The pay-off is not usually worth the time invested, especially for what are eventually just nonsense words—that is, these are not words that merit taking the time to illustrate.

A similar reinforcer would be to have students construct their own "affixionaries," in this case *prefixionaries*. An in-service teacher created one; the prefixes were listed alphabetically, one per page. She made class books, laminated, accessible to all children. Each page would have a definition at the top, followed by words using the targeted affix and a few representative sentences. There were several blank pages for students to access if they chose to add something over the course of the year.

Suffixes

A total of around ten suffixes and their variants account for a large majority of meanings. These suffixes do not include inflectional endings, such as -ed or -ing. Teachers might, of course, list the suffixes, meanings, and examples.

Suffix	*Meaning*	*Examples*
-al	referring to	fanatical, visual, sexual, comical
-er, -or	someone who does	orator, liberator, monitor, mentor, fighter
-ian	someone who is expert at	psychometrician, tactician, physician
-ist	someone who does	violinist, arsonist
-ment	result of, act of	punishment, torment, abandonment
-ward	in the direction of	forward, leeward, backward, skyward

As stated earlier, you can create affixionaries, in this case *suffixionaries*. Suffixes frequently signify the part of speech the "whole word" will be, and sometimes they add further meaning. Some suffixes are better understood not as having a particular meaning but as expressing grammar or syntax. These suffixes enable one to express an idea in many different ways by using the variation of the key word that fits the sentence structure. For example, consider the following sentences:

1. Suzanne is very *happy*.
2. Suzanne is playing *happily*.
3. Suzanne's *happiness* was disturbed by the mean dog.

The key word "happy" was altered to fit the sentence structure. Without hitting children with too many rules, the teacher can still provide targeted instruction, pointing out that in the first sentence "happy" is used as an adjective; in the second sentence the function is that of an adverb (and it is very reliable in terms of rule, teaching that -ly often signifies an adverb); and in sentence number three, -ness was added so that the root word could "morph" into a noun.

A frame such as the above could be provided to help children manipulate the suffixes in other words. In the following example, the students would be asked to supply forms of "sad."

1. Jamaale is _____.
2. Jamaale talked _____.
3. Jamaale's _____ was due to his poor report card.

As always, good teachers take it to the application level and have students create the frames for others to solve. This brings us to a genuine question. We all know what inept means, as opposed to adept. If one is average at a task, can he be described as "ept"?

SYLLABICATION RULES

The teaching of syllabication rules is somewhat controversial. The *concept* of syllabication is fine, and we still see young children merrily clapping or tapping in order to reinforce the notion. But rules, according to some, may not be worth the time-cost. Syllables sometimes are part of phonics lessons because syllabication affects vowel sounds, and sometimes they may be included as part of spelling or English lessons. There is no consensus on various lists of syllabication rules, and some of the rules have quite a few exceptions. Below, FYI, are four syllabication rules. These are not "musts" by any means. If they help your students, use them, but get them back into context quickly. These four were adapted from Fry, Kress, and Fountoukidis (2000, p. 43).

Rule 1. VCV: A consonant between two vowels tends to go with the second vowel:

spoken = spo`-ken

prevent = pre`-vent

defer = de`-fer

Rule 2. VCCV: Divide two consonants between two vowels unless they are a blend or a digraph:

batter = bat-ter

plaster = plas-ter

combine = com-bine

deflate = de-flate

Rule 3. Affixes: Prefixes always form separate syllables, and suffixes sometimes do:

dis-con-tent

pre-vent

re-lapse

tri-dent

The suffix -y tends to pick up the consonant before it, and form a separate syllable:

migh-ty

faul-ty

stea-my

The suffix -ed tends to form a separate syllable when it follows a root that ends in t or d:

vent-ed versus stopped

end-ed versus shelled

relat-ed versus parked

Rule 4. Compounds: Always divide compound words.

base-ball

bus-boy

It has been said that the application of phonics is easy, if you already know what the word is. Syllabication rules are kind of similar, but they can be helpful in learning words by analogy. Keep rule teaching to a minimum. It is better to teach to the application level, and to help kids to "notice" patterns and trends. Remember, if a child can complete a worksheet, then she doesn't need it.

Fisher and Frey (2007b) provide an excellent description of a school-wide "words of the week" (WOW) program at Harrison Middle School. They describe the articulation and planning necessary to choose five words each week. In choosing the words, each "set" of five has a common prefix, suffix, or root. The intention, as it should always be, is to turn control over to the students. The following is an example:

Week 1	**Week 2**	**Week 3**	**Week 4**
Suffix: *-ist*	Root: *-cent*	Prefix: *mal-*	Root: *-ortho*
One who does something	*Center*	*Bad or Evil*	*Straight or Correct*
pharmacist	eccentric	malnutrition	orthopedic
philanthropist	egocentric	malicious	orthodontist
communist	centralized	malevolent	orthodox
artist	decentralize	malnutrition	unorthodox
psychologist	concentric	malpractice	
pugilist	centrifuge	malignant	

All of the teachers in the school then reinforce the chosen words. By my calculations, that would be 180 words in a three-grade middle level career.

SPELLING (A QUICK TREATMENT)

Spelling is the most researched area of the language arts, yet it is still fraught with controversy. Spelling is a surface structure of writing, and as such is tangible and is noticed by parents and the public.

Children's knowledge of English orthography (rules of spelling) develops in fairly predictable stages (Bear, Invernizzi, Templeton, & Johnson, 2007) and experts agree that some spelling errors are related to children's misunderstandings of how meaning impacts on English spelling. Structural analysis study helps with spelling, so we will limit our discussion to that relationship. Blachowicz and Fisher (2010) have suggested a possible four-stage sequence of instruction that includes the following:

1. Silent/sounded consonants in related words:
   sign/signal
   malign/malignant
   muscle/muscular
   damn/damnation
   column/columnist
   These word pairs are examples of roots that have silent consonants, which are then sounded when a suffix is added.
2. Vowel and consonants alternations:
   digest—digestion
   clinic—clinician

divide—division
cave—cavity
compose—composition
definite—finite
conventional—convene
grammar—grammatical
Sabbath—sabbatical

There are many alternations, where different forms of vowels and consonants change fairly regularly—the examples here are representative of what can occur.

3. Absorbed or assimilated prefixes. This occurs when a prefix loses some of its letters when it joins a root word. The letters are absorbed by the root word, which doubles its initial consonant:

ad + tend = attended (to)
ad + fect = affect
com + respond = correspond (with)
com + rupt = corrupt
in + mature = immature (not)
in + legal = illegal
ob + cupy = occupy (to)
ob + pose = oppose
sub + port = support (under)
sub + fix = suffix

4. Roots and combining forms. Use cubes, cut-up individual letters, roots, and affixes. The cubes may be purchased, or borrowed, from games like Boggle. The affixes, roots, and individual letters can be written on cards and laminated. It's very much like Cunningham's (1995) "making words." You may do this with small groups, but it can be done whole group, using the SMART board. For example, children might have the following:

re-	-cycle	-er
uni-	-phone	-ness
tele-	-graph	-able
pre-	-happy	
un-	-season	

Have the children manipulate the given affixes and roots to make words. Start by being pretty explicit: for example, "Take the root word happy and add a prefix to make a whole word that means 'sad.' Now add a suffix to the word you have created to make it into a noun. Be careful, you are going to have to change a letter."

Be sure to see the second edition of *Words Their Way: Word Sorts for Syllables and Affixes Spellers* (F. Johnston, Invernizzi, Bear, & Templeton,

2009). This useful collection is designed for students in grades 3–8. The responses from the field have been overwhelmingly positive.

ETYMOLOGY

If teachers can help students to become interested and curious about words and word study, the motivation will go a long way. Studying and exploring the origins of words can be fun and motivating. Word learning does not have to be drudgery! It's fascinating how our language is such an eclectic collection of words borrowed from around the world. If we can model the interest and give kids the permission to take their time and explore interesting words and their origins, the payoffs are potentially great. According to Johnson (2001), English word origins can be traced to more than 120 languages; for example:

bandage (French)	polo (Tibetan)
charisma (Greek)	sauna (Finnish)
geyser (Icelandic)	waffle (Dutch)
hammock (Haitian)	yoga (Sanskrit)
kayak (Inuit)	

The ever-changing qualities of our language are captured in chapter 9, from clipping to blending to dialect to idioms—and more. We even make up words to take the place of words that "escape" us (e.g., doohickey, gizmo, thingamajig).

Plenty of words have come into our language, for example, through mythology:

Odyssey—The long, arduous journey of Odysseus has been generalized into a long trip.

Titans—The race of giants in Greek mythology has given us the word "Titanic."

Narcissistic—Narcissus fell in love with his own reflection. We use the word "narcissistic" to describe someone who is self-absorbed.

Psyche—Psyche was made immortal; now she relates to the human soul or spirit in words like psychology, psychic.

Tantalus—This Greek king's name gave us the word "tantalize."

Sirens—These temptresses in the Odyssey lured ships to destruction with their singing; their name is now generalized to mean seduction.

Be sure, as well, to see the appendices in this book for websites, resources, and various and other tidbits you may wish to share with your students as you move them along the continuum to becoming eager, cheerful, and willing word detectives. Following are some activities that require your students to home in on word parts. After some direct instruction, these games can be used for reinforcement. In the best situations, students either create the game, or add components. There are many game-like activities available for you to be flexible in doing word work. Here are a few more game-like activities:

WORD GAMES FOCUSING ON WORD PARTS

Compound It

Present individuals or groups with lists of words; have them form as many compound words as possible. This can be done competitively, in a timed fashion if you prefer. Examples are brainstorm, rainstorm, sandstorm.

back	cook	note	sail	bone
boat	drop	play	sand	brain
board	mail	rail	stone	pad
book	man	rain	rack	fall
box	mate	road	hat	block
coat	milk	room	wish	storm

As always, talk and sharing is what matters. Word knowledge increases, as do skimming and scanning skills.

Triple Threat

This is an association activity. The object is to find a word that "unites" three other words.

___day	___load	___master	(pay)
___man	___dog	___word	(watch)
___state	___wear	___done	(under)
class___	check___	play___	(mate)
___eat	___sleep	___work	(over)
___marc	___fall	___long	(night)
bed___	board___	ante___	(room)

The teacher goes for variety by providing four parts. Once children are familiar with the format, leave blanks and have students fill them in:

_____ head _____ sleep   (over)
short _____ rain _____   (fall)

In the first sample, two of the words that link are "overhead" and "oversleep." The students have to come up with others: overnight, overdraft, overdue.

Vocabulary Squares

These are sound pedagogically, for they include a visual dimension in support of a word's definition and the reader's personal association with the word (Readence, Bean, & Baldwin, 1989). They are particularly good for concrete words. This strategy is flexible, beginning with division of a piece of paper into quarters (see figures 7.1a and 7.1b).

We have covered the notion that naturally occurring context alone, unrepeated, is not very efficient for learning new words. Additionally, definitions have their drawbacks—when children are asked what a "chalice" is, for example, they might say, "Well, it's like a glass." What is nice about vocabulary squares is they can be customized and manipulated to give the requisite overlapping. Some examples of the four parts are

1. keyword;
2. word in context;

Figure 7.1.   Vocabulary Squares

3. definition;
4. cue/trigger; or

1. keyword;
2. cue/trigger;
3. what it is like;
4. characteristics.

The combination the students use depends on their grade level and the part of speech that the keyword is. Intentional redundancy means purposeful repetition. For example, a word of the week from mid-September may reappear on the word wall in November and again in Shazam! games in April (see figures 7.2a, 7.2b, 7.2c, and 7.2d).

It is up to the learners and the teacher what goes in which quadrant, but the more personalized they are, the more learning will be retained. Different words lend themselves to different strategies—"giraffe" is concrete and easy to draw, whereas "anticipation" is not. Use salient word parts because they're "transportable," but some words only have one part that's a good fit. Examples and non-examples can be great and definitions also work.

Verbalizing and explication must abound. Some students may get frustrated with having to make choices. Depending on your class, it may be wise

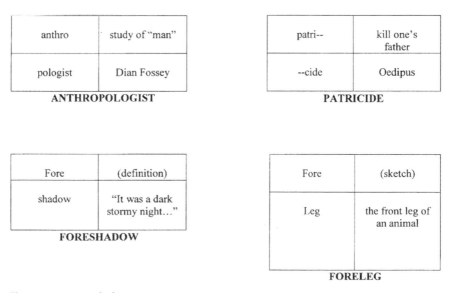

Figure 7.2.   Vocabulary Squares

to structure the activity tightly in the beginning until the students grow accustomed to the latitude you provide.

Word parts do merit instructional time! Please be sure to provide your students with variety, and please remember that *targeted* instruction is the key. Keep this aspect of word work quick and concise.

Chapter Eight

Using Dictionaries and Other Tools of Reference

The covers of this book are too far apart.

—Ambrose Bierce

CHRISTY

Christy DiValerio teaches ninth grade English. She is young and idealistic, working hard and learning about her students and their needs. She sees the dictionary (the old fashioned kind) as a critical tool that her students have access to, but she believes that some modern conveniences (particularly the spell checker) promote bad habits. In their formal, typed papers her students consider proofing their work to be running the spell checker and ascertaining that all the words in place are spelled correctly—but she has found that the children have little concern as to whether the correct *word is spelled correctly; that is, homophones are used inappropriately.*

Additionally, Christy is finding that the electronic thesauri are contributing to her pupils trying to use impressive vocabulary when a simpler word will do. As Christmas vacation nears, Christy comes up with an edict for the rest of the year. Starting in January, all papers will be written in class, by hand, without the computer. All papers must be proofed by the author and at least two other students in the class. When the final draft is executed, all papers with any misspellings and/or misuses of homophones (e.g., then for than, plane for plain, as well as your, there, its, and so forth) will automatically receive an F.

Do you think that Christy is being a bit heavy-handed? What about the repercussions in regards to the students taking risks with language? And what about time-cost factors (with all that class time being devoted to writing mechanics, will some valuable skills and strategies be left uncovered)? Who said that teaching is an easy job?

A colleague read in a popular magazine that while at preparatory school, George W. Bush was urged by his mother to use the thesaurus so that he'd have better word choice and a wider-ranging vocabulary. According to the article, when writing a personal narrative, George W. penned "lacerates ran down my cheek" to describe himself crying. It seems that he found a synonym for the homograph "tear"—meaning to rip—when he in fact wanted the synonym to fit "tear," salty wet ones.

Dictionaries, thesauri, and other tools can be very useful for young (and old and middle-aged) readers and writers. Whereas chapter 1 might have overdone it in lampooning the misuses of the dictionary, in this section the upside of these aids to word learning will be accentuated. Learning a definition is sometimes a good way of making meaning.

Dictionaries can be used much more effectively than the old "look up the definition" (which definition?) and "use it in an original sentence" way. As you shall soon see, dictionaries are of little use when it comes to unknown words. Remember the Blachowicz and Fisher (2010) metaphor regarding word learning to be more akin to a dimmer switch than an on/off switch? Children can start off with having a "whiff of the word," a very vague notion of its meaning(s)—and they can gradually refine their understanding of words. In addition to providing examples (and non-examples) of a word, overlapping a definition can help a child to internalize a word, to gain a deep understanding.

DICTIONARIES

When one wants to look up a word to find its meaning, spelling, or pronunciation, the dictionary is the tool of choice. The dictionary is a book of meanings, multiple meanings, pronunciations, spellings, grammatical information, and etymologies—usually organized alphabetically. According to Johnson (2001), dictionaries have been in existence for about four thousand years. The first dictionaries were used to help travelers translate one language into another. The precursor of modern English dictionaries was a Chinese compilation (Johnson, 2001).

Two important English language dictionaries were produced—one by Dr. Samuel Johnson, the famous British lexicographer (1775), and one by an American, Noah Webster (1824). Then came the most ambitious of all dictionaries, the *Oxford English Dictionary* (*OED*), published in 1928. Webster added (and added, and added!) an American English dictionary that would outdo Johnson's version. The *OED* took on a life of its own. Work on it commenced in 1857, and was not published in its entirety until 1928, and reissued in 1933. The *OED* defined nearly 415,000 word forms! A twenty-volume second edition was published in 1989 (in its 21,730 pages, it topped out at 615,100 word forms and used 2,436,600 quotations [Berg, 1993]).

Types of Dictionaries

Johnson (2001) categorizes dictionaries into four types: monolingual of a language, bilingual (or more) for translation, single function dictionaries, and single topic dictionaries, such as medical dictionaries (p. 78). Dictionaries can be further classified according to their intended audiences: by age and/ or experience (e.g., elementary school, intermediate, college) or profession/ specialty.

Monolingual general dictionaries are the most commonly used they come in all sizes and contain just about everything a learner might possibly need: the meanings of any word that needs to be understood, the spelling of any word that needs to be written, and the pronunciation of any word that needs to be spoken.

The following section is concerned with using the dictionary to gain new or enhanced understanding of meaning, as opposed to the spelling or pronunciation functions. It's akin to a refrigerator repairman. First he's got to recognize what part among many is not functioning properly, then he's got to go in and fix it, then he's got to test it to see that it's working.

How to Use a Dictionary

Scholfield (1982) listed a seven step process, which Blachowicz and Fisher (2010) reduced/collapsed into five steps:

1. knowing when you don't know a word
2. knowing how to locate the word
3. knowing the parts of a dictionary entry
4. choosing from among multiple meanings
5. applying the meaning

Unfortunately, dictionary "instruction" in schools has not normally in-cluded the metacognitive first step, and not much teaching (just assigning) has been done around the fifth step, either, so the emphasis has been on the middle three (rather mechanical) steps. Yet the most important thing to teach students is how to ascertain when the dictionary is needed.

Knowing When to Use a Dictionary

Blachowicz and Fisher (2010) use the concept of definition model adapted from Schwartz and Raphael (1985). This visual organizer helps children develop a clear idea of what "knowing" a word entails, for middle level stu-dents are able to compare what they know about a word with what they *need* to know. The next big step will then be, if the student recognizes the need to know, having the drive and determination (the striving domain, conation) to take the time and energy to "look it up." But first things first; back to concept of definition.

Chapter 4 presented a concept of definition graphic for the word "assassin" that included the key word and three questions: What is it? What is it like? What are some examples? The thoroughness with which you teach a concept of definition map depends on your purpose and how far along your students are (see figure 8.1 for a sample map). The number of steps and the sequence are not sacrosanct, but generally go as follows:

1. Introduce the visual on the chalkboard, overhead projector, or SMART Board—do easy examples together—turn control over to students, gradu-ally moving to more complex words.
2. Model for students how to use maps to write a definition—have students use their own maps to write their own definitions.
3. Model for students how knowing the component parts of the map helps you "know when you know" the meaning—model this in a passage.
4. Have the whole group read a passage with difficult vocabulary inter-spersed—have them choose words they know they don't know.
5. Model, using the dictionary, how to complete the map in order to get them closer to full comprehension (Blachowicz & Fisher, 2010).

As always, teachers must weigh time-cost factors. It should also be remem-bered that it is fairly expensive time-wise, and possibly impractical, for time is often a mitigating factor in vocabulary teaching. Additionally, these maps typically work well for nouns, but do not "fit" as nicely for adjectives and ad-verbs. Which leads us to a different type of map, the basic word map, shown in figure 8.2 (adapted from Blachowicz & Fisher, 2010).

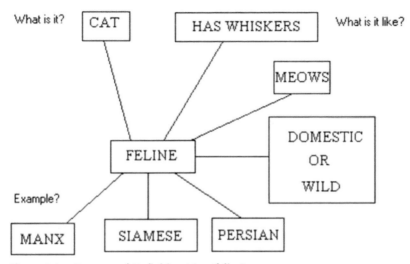

Figure 8.1. Concept of Definition Map (feline)

For the word map in figure 8.2, the key word is "elated." To help the students develop a thorough understanding of the word, in partnership with the teacher they generate a synonym, an antonym, an example, and a non-example. In order to delineate examples and non-examples, students must be pretty clear on significant characteristics. It is also easier to come up with

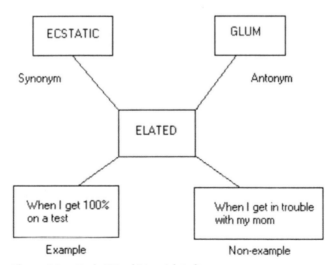

Figure 8.2. Basic Word Map (elated)

synonyms and antonyms for non-nouns. This word map is definitely easier to complete for non-nouns, and is generally more flexible and quicker to use.

If the key word were "cactus," for example, it would be difficult to come up with synonyms and antonyms. A cactus is a type of succulent, but that would constitute a subordinate relationship, and cactus and succulent are not synonyms. Similar problems arise with pinpointing antonyms. Depending upon the teacher's purpose and the needs of children, the preceding maps should be readily available for helping children "know when they know" or "know when they don't know."

Knowing How to Locate a Word

Children learn ABC order (aka alphabetizing) early in their schooling. This skill is a necessary precursor, of course, to using a dictionary well. For fourth and fifth graders, as well as English language learners, the creation of a class picture dictionary is a useful activity for teaching various dictionary concepts: alphabetical order, beginning letter sounds, and the general organization of the tool.

Of course, after they have completed the class dictionary, students can be involved in creating their own individual dictionaries. These should be geared toward helping students find difficult-to-spell words for writing. You might include a section for structure words (there, is, of, an, were, where, etc.) that only lists these high-frequency words—there is little use in trying to define, give non-examples, antonyms and the like for these words. And you'll be hard-pressed to draw or find a picture of a "the."

The content words (aka academic vocabulary) are another matter—although they occur much less frequently than the structure words, they are concrete and salient and lend themselves nicely to mapping, dictionary entry, and various exercises. Be sure to allow students to *talk about* the words they're adding and (depending upon district philosophy as well as professional beliefs) decide upon parameters for correct spelling. Even proponents of developmental spelling (aka invented spelling) believe that dictionary spellings should be letter perfect.

After alphabetization, the most useful skill to have students practice is the use of guide words. These exercises are common in workbooks, for they're not very difficult to produce! Students might have a set or sets of guide words—for example, "carpet–cavalry," "green–grove"—and a list of words, and must decide which word(s) from the list would belong under the appropriate guide words. The research on worksheet-type guide word activities is quite equivocal. It is strongly recommended that teaching of guide words be embedded in actual, purposeful dictionary use, rather than as a "canned" activity.

The Parts of a Dictionary

Because of space constraints, dictionaries have brief definitions that often require the use of difficult terminology, as well as complex word choice. How frustrating it is for students to go through the two steps presented earlier: to ascertain that they need to know a word (at a cost!) and then locate the word (at more cost!), only to stall at the third step due to technical difficulties with the nuances of dictionary conventions. Below are several noted difficulties with dictionary definitions adapted by McKeown (1990). Three problems that she notes are weak differentiation, vague language, and disjointed definitions.

1. *Weak differentiation* occurs when the major characteristics are not salient enough to distinguish the key word from other similar words—from an earlier example, although "balmy" means comfortably warm, it would not be an apt descriptor for a meal; likewise, "livid," meaning white hot, would not be used to describe a kiln or a cooking range.
2. *Vague language* contributes to fuzzy understanding and unclear definitions—such entries make it very difficult for a child to ascertain what words go together appropriately.
3. *Disjointed definitions* may not connect various aspects of multi-meaning words, and may require a great deal of background knowledge on the part of the students. Teachers must be sensitive to the bewilderment of weak readers who are left to navigate through too much unfamiliar print with too little help.

Obstacles such as these three can be either temporarily avoided or dealt with head on. In a manner somewhat akin to the control provided by decodable text, the teacher can limit instruction to tackling word entries children can easily understand. Lots of teacher modeling and support are required so that students can flexibly use appropriate strategies for finding meaning. In fact, the formulaic messages implicit in some of the numbered steps are presented here—even though they are often collapsed and omit some less-essential information, they may be too linear (yet there are both teachers and students who are much more comfortable with recipes).

The motivational aspects of game-like activities using dictionaries are familiar. For example, many of us remember adult dictionary games—there was one where words were drawn and people/players tried to pass off realistic-sounding but absolutely bogus definitions. By the way, the surest way to get students to voluntarily use dictionaries (and thesauri) is through the use of crossword puzzles.

Choosing among Multiple Meanings

Students are very likely to choose the briefest definition for a word. When they are not invested in words, brevity is the watchword. When students locate words of their choosing, in meaningful context, an appropriate, accurate dictionary definition is much more probable. Bannon, Fisher, Pozzi, and Wessell (1990) developed a cross-checking procedure (called PAVE) that requires students to cross-check a word's meaning with the context in which it appears. The components of the strategy make up the acronym in PAVE: p*rediction*, a*ssociation*, v*erification*, and e*valuation*. It is a very valuable mnemonic—let's go through the strategy and share an adapted PAVE map. This is significantly modified and enhanced from the original version.

Stacy, a young graduate student, developed the following modified/enhanced PAVE. Here are the steps:

1. Students choose key words. They quickly mark them, and come back to them later.
2. Students write the word(s) in context. They are instructed how to use ellipses.
3. Next, they write the word alone.
4. Students then *predict* the meaning.
5. Then they write an original sentence, using the key word (*associative*).
6. Students then *verify* the definition in the dictionary.
7. The students write a "better" sentence.
8. Students, next, *evaluate* how they've done, and fill in the bottom of the modified PAVE form (see figure 8.3) to give themselves hooks to aid in remembering. The bottom section (see sample PAVE organizers) add on concepts from vocabulary squares (see figure 8.3). This section is intentionally quite flexible, depending on the words chosen.

Stacy had devised a system where the PAVE map frames are written on both sides of 8 ½ × 11-inch, three-hole paper. The students are then required to collect their words in three-ring binders. A visit to her class revealed the effectiveness of her methodology. Three words were done as a whole class, using the frame on the overhead projector, allowing the students to nominate words. Of course, a flip chart or the blackboard will suffice. At any rate, we went through the process with students filling out their own copies. We had a couple of designated dictionary checkers—the verification stage is very important.

MODIFIED PAVE:
(Predict, Associate, Verify, Evaluate)

Your Name: _Tammy_   Source _Old Yeller_   Date _3·10·xx_ .

Word in Context: _I was plenty scared of that hydrophobia plague ..._

Your Word Alone: _hydrophobic_

Your Predicted Definition: _fear of water_

Your Original Sentence: _Sam had both claustrophobia and hydrophobia_

Dictionary Definition: _rabies_

Your Better Sentence: _Raccoons are often carriers of rabies_

Key Words	Visual Cue
fear water quarantine	 foam
Antonyms (or what it's not like)	**Synonyms** (or what it's like)
safe	dangerous contagious

Figure 8.3. PAVE

Applying the Meaning

Students have necessarily gone to a lot of work to get to this stage. Children still need to apply that meaning either to comprehend their reading or to communicate clearly in written discourse. When children get to the dictionary, they sometimes find that none of the meanings fit exactly in the sentence context, so the "best" meaning needs to be chosen.

After several think-alouds, have students demonstrate some thinking aloud of their own, either in small groups or before the whole class. The goal (use the term "gradually relinquish control" a great deal) is to model and practice just *enough* to transfer the locus of control to the students. Our best and our brightest can tune in and tune out, and do not find inauthentic exercises to be very fulfilling.

The dictionary has gotten plenty of treatment in this chapter, and the thesaurus was gone over in some detail earlier in chapter 6. Many publishers now distribute dictionaries that are geared to particular grade levels. These are more child friendly than the bigger, broader-based commercial dictionaries and often include helpful lists, tips, homonyms, high-frequency words, and the like.

Additionally, these little booklets often include space for students to add their own notations, additions, and personal records. These useful resources recognize the developmental needs of children and focus on the "less is more" principle, with an emphasis on children being able to find what they need in an expeditious fashion. Most of these are reasonably priced at around two dollars or so, with discounts for bulk purchases.

Following are two reminders about these mini-dictionaries. Even though they're student friendly and streamlined as opposed to regular dictionaries, you still need to explicitly teach children how to use them. Dictionaries such as these are useful tools for word study time and for certain stages of process writing. Additionally, it is best to not introduce these at the very beginning of the school year—wait a month or two so that students get the notion of meaning first and taking risks as writers. You don't want your pupils to over-rely on them.

All of the major dictionary publishers now produce electronic dictionaries, which range greatly in complexity. As alluded to earlier, these are mixed blessings. Due to the power of CD-ROM, massive amounts of information can be stored and easily accessed. Some of the electronic dictionaries pronounce words out loud, thereby negating the need for traditional phonetic symbols. Other types allow users to compile glossaries of specialized terms. As students continue to do more and more word processing, they have access to spell-checking programs and electronic thesauruses and dictionaries.

The spell-checking is clearly more convenient in electronic fashion, but students will need to be responsible for *proofing* properly when executing a final draft—running the spell-checker does not take care of meaning, homonym issues, missing words, and the like. Just as talking books (books on tape) and reading online have not replaced paper versions, electronic dictionaries and electronic thesauruses will not "replace" hard copies any time soon!

OTHER VOCABULARY TOOLS

Fairly complete treatment has been given to the dictionary as an aid in word learning. Additionally, the thesaurus has been discussed in chapter 4. In the final section of this chapter, a few reminders are provided about some other useful tools. These are sometimes called "features of text." In my experience, unless teachers monitor closely, students often misuse or ignore these valuable tools.

Features of Text: Glossaries

A glossary is a specialized sub-dictionary that is customized to a particular text/context. For example, the word "interest" will be defined specifically related to "money earned on an investment" in a mathematics textbook, or in a text relating to economics. That is, the many other meanings of interest will not be included. Similar to the "typical to technical" strategy, students need to discern which meaning is the appropriate meaning. The glossary is designed to aid in that process.

The glossary is a courtesy, which makes the text more considerate for students. However, unless they are explicitly taught how to use the glossary, students often fail to access it on their own. Sometimes they try; sometimes they don't truly need the glossary. Some students find a major disconnect between the words they actually need to know and the words provided by the glossary. Someone who was presumably smarter "knew" the needs of all students.

Features of Text: Italics and Pronunciation Guides

Students usually have trouble using pronunciation guides, and they often fail to pay attention to italics. Depending upon the age and maturity of your students, you need to slow them down and explicitly teach them how to use these tools.

The most common tools for vocabulary enrichment and spelling (namely, thesauri and dictionaries; mainly dictionaries) must be used strategically. As outlined earlier, students need a variety of word leaning strategies, and these must be used together. In general, we want student independence, but we recognize the need to provide necessary scaffolding. When a word is unknown to students and the teacher's consistent reply is, "Look it up," to some students it's a dismissive answer (i.e., "You figure it out"; "I don't have the time or the inclination"; "I'm here to teach, you're here to learn"; "Don't bug me"). It's very much akin to the admonition to "sound it out" at the word recognition level. They would if they could.

Remember, vocabulary development is a gradual process. As outlined previously, after many encounters with a word, a gradually more precise grasp of the concept unfolds. As students encounter increasingly demanding reading loads, they'll continue to require support in enhancing their own vocabulary—building strategies that clearly include the appropriate, targeted use of reference tools such as the dictionary. Remember, as well, to explicitly teach italics, bold print, and other "courtesies" provided by authors.

Chapter Nine

Serendipity

Her vocabulary was as bad as, like, whatever.

—Anonymous

ERIK AS JOE COCKER

Last school day before Thanksgiving vacation. Tom Freed's seventh graders are playing charades. Teams are picked; each side makes up the stipulated categories for the other team to present and solve: book titles, movie titles, and song titles. The students are very excited, warming to the task. Mr. Freed is the time keeper and final arbiter of correct answers.

Erik is up. He reads the slip of paper, makes an awful face, thinks a little, and springs into action by diving onto the floor (he has the novel Island of the Blue Dolphins *[O'Dell, 1960] to convey to his teammates in sixty seconds or less). Just as Erik hits the floor, the principal walks in. He sees all of Erik's teammates crowding and craning, shouting out their answers. It looks like Erik is doing a bad imitation of Joe Cocker, for he is trying to be a "dolphin," rocking in the "waves"—humping along on the floor. . . . The principal turns and heads out the door.*

This chapter is devoted to word play. The students in this vignette were overtly having fun. Your goal should be to try to have pleasurable experiences with words daily. Students can learn new words and expand their knowledge of partially known words, exploring and refining. Be sure to adapt the activities that follow to suit the needs and predilections of your students.

Whereas many of the content area strategies presented can fit into the narrative section, most of the "fun stuff" presented here clearly fits in this chapter. These word play aspects are very motivating and do result in greater word retention than some of the more "serious" methods. Susan Ohanion (2002) has argued compellingly for the need for students to "stand by words," for the importance of attitude and disposition to learn words as opposed to the traditional drill and practice of the past. Her book is filled with fun activities for teachers and students.

That being said, playful use of vocabulary is best coupled with the self-collection principles. Middle level learners are quick to take ownership of these word play activities, once they are modeled and demystified. And *that* being said, here are some playful choices for word work that children enjoy, replete with examples.

PUNS

The pun is the lowest form of humor. It's also very much enjoyed by children young and old. From Shakespeare (Mercutio, when mortally wounded, quipped, "Ask for me tomorrow, and you shall find me a grave man") to contemporary writers, people can be extremely clever in their word play.

An effective structure for punning is to use Tom Swifties. Tom Swift was an early boy genius/radio character, and a sort of Jimmy Neutron prototype and predecessor. *And* he was a punster. So simply tell the students a little about him, and then model a bit:

"I'm going to practice my archery," said Tom with a quiver.
"That car's a lemon," said Tom sourly.
"There goes Captain Hook," said Tom offhandedly.
"I'm going to change your grade," the teacher remarked.

Next, pause and delve, having the students identify the puns in the sentences you have provided. Here is a reconstruction of how you might think aloud with your students:

> Okay gang, try this one. Remember, we are looking at a sentence, for now, that ends in an adverb that has a double meaning, telling how Tom said or did something. Here we go. "Don't sit in the back of the boat ," said Tom _____
> _____. So I think of the word "sit," and play around in my head with squat, squatting, seat . . . no, it must have to do with the back of a boat. Let's see. Stern.

Sternly! That must be it. The stern is the back of a boat and someone can speak sternly. It means kind of mean and strict.

Here's another one, it's pretty hard. "I wish I had written down what I need at the store," said Tom _____. Hmmmmmmm. When you write down what you need at the store, it's a list. Listly? Listingly? It has to be list-lessly. When you don't have friends, you are friendless, when you lack care, you're careless.

Then invite the students to take over. The puns are often adverbs, but can be verbs, and nouns.

"I'm losing weight," said Tom lightly.
"I'll take the long way home," said Tom indirectly.
"I'm taking a trip around the world," said Tom globally.
"That poison ivy sure does itch!" said Tom rashly.

Students also enjoy illustrating puns. A "puntoon" is an example of a port-manteau word, combining pun and cartoon, but more on word blends later.

IDIOMS

Fred Gwynne was an actor who wrote books on idioms, including *The King Who Rained* (1970) and *A Chocolate Moose for Dinner* (1976). Idioms cause confusion for second language learners and early readers, for their literal meanings are often confounding. For example, when someone has a bee in her bonnet, the meaning is more complex than the surface structure of the words. Idioms are fun to illustrate. They're also a device used in the Amelia Bedelia series (Parish & Parish).

These are appropriate for elementary-aged children in particular. Be care-ful, as always, of time-cost factors. A class book is a nice reinforcer, but then move on, for you have bigger fish to fry . . . if you play your cards right. Sorry, I couldn't resist.

PALINDROMES

Palindromes are words or phrases or sentences that are identical when read either forward or backwards. So the words "deed" or "noon" or "level" would be palindromes. A famous phrase that is a palindrome would be what Na-poleon may have uttered: "Able I was, ere I saw Elba." What kind of mind sits around and thinks of palindromes? But there are entire books written on palindromes! Following are some examples of palindromic phrases and sentences:

drowsy sword
Neil, an alien
Was it a car or a cat I saw?
Marge lets Norah see Sharon's telegram.

Palindromes can also be presented to children in riddle form. Give the children the riddle, let them supply the palindrome.

gently touch Patricia = tap pat
sleep in a metal frying dish = nap pan
when friends strike each other = pals slap
scarecrow's skin bumps = straw warts

Again, don't spend inordinate amounts of time. An occasional treatment is adequate.

CORRUPTIONS

These are dialectic pronunciations that have made it into our language in their mispronounced states. These are difficult. Start by giving older children the corrupted form, then have them decide what "proper" word was the genesis:

critter = creature
vittles = victuals
varmint = vermin
crick = creek
munch = mange

These examples are rather obtuse and rare. Do not spend a great deal of time with these, but your students may surprise you with their interest.

SPOONERISMS

The Reverend William Archibald Spooner, dean of New College, Oxford, was a learned man, but he often got his mords wixed, er, words mixed, that is. Nobody knows how many "spoonerisms" were really made by him, but ostensibly he

- referred to Queen Victoria as "our queer old dean";
- said that "the Lord is a shoving leopard";
- told a nervous bride groom that "it is kisstomery to cuss the bride."

Other Spoonerisms include "blushing crow," "beery wenches," and "Is the bean dizzy?" for crushing blow, weary benches, and Is the dean busy? respectively. Spoonerisms are a bridge to discussion of malapropisms, the most notable perpetrator being Yogi Berra, who spoke of "déjà vu all over again" and once said "when you come to a fork in the road, take it."

PUZZLES/COLLECTION/SHARING OF VOCABULARY

As mentioned earlier, various puzzle formats increase student interest and motivation. When students have collected a number of good words revolving around a theme or topic, have them incorporate the vocabulary into a word bank, and then use the words to make word searches or crossword puzzles. What is important is that the students produce these products for their classmates to solve, giving them the stamp of authenticity.

HINK PINKS

These were introduced in chapter 1. (Remember the sinister minister and the funny bunny and the smitten kitten? You had a very difficult one to solve.) They are presented in riddle form and are fun for children to illustrate. Hink pinks (I have no idea where the term came from) are one-syllable rhyming word pairs.

An overweight feline is a "fat cat."
A person who steals steaks is "a beef thief."

A hinky pinky is a two-syllable rhyming pair.

A better café is a "finer diner."
A loud boom box one can hear through the wall is a "plaster blaster."
A weighty group of quails is a "heavy bevy."

Hinkety pinketys are three-syllable rhymes.

The okay to take something away is "removal approval."
A frightening taking of weapons is an "alarming disarming."

Finally, hinketyty pinketytys are four-syllable rhymes. Here is the answer to the hinketyty pinketyty previously mentioned: A New Yorker's booze cabinet is a knickerbocker liquorlocker!!

Here are more for your students.

	Answers
1. a cucumber for five cents	*nickel pickle*
2. a tuba with a hole in it	*torn horn*
3. a person who puts saltines in a box	*cracker packer*
4. a runner in the snow	*winter sprinter*
5. the home of a rodent	*mouse house*
6. an overweight feline	*fat cat*
7. a crime done with a newspaper	*paper caper*
8. a fake timepiece	*mock clock*
9. a male doll	*toy boy*
10. a drinking apparatus in the Rockies	*mountain fountain*
11. a corner for keeping reading material	*book nook*
12. an automobile in which liquid refreshments are served	*car bar*
13. a truck to carry recyclables	*can van*
14. not getting to an appointment on time	*late date*
15. a vehicle for carrying muddy soil	*muck truck*
16. a budget motel	*fin inn*
17. an insect living in a maple	*bee tree*
18. an insect living in a carpet	*rug bug*
19. a child's bed	*tot cot*
20. a child's means of transportation	*tyke trike*

See appendix 2-E for more examples.

EPONYMS

Eponyms are words that "come from" proper nouns, usually people or places. In most cases, the proper noun is generalized/popularized into a common noun. A simple example is the word atlas. In Greek mythology, Atlas was the giant of strength, and many books of maps and geography pictured Atlas holding up the world. Eventually they called these map books "atlases."

Another example is "hooligan," the common noun meaning a rowdy, unruly person, which was derived from a notorious Irish family of the same name. Start the children off with several examples. What you are having the students do, by the way, is a vocabulary *activity*. The students are actively engaged in searching for eponyms, and they learn new words.

bologna: the sausage, named after the Italian city
pasteurized: named for French scientist Louis Pasteur
sandwich: named after the Earl of Sandwich, who did not want to leave the gambling table to eat, so he had a servant bring him meat between two pieces of bread
frankfurter:
hamburger:
macadam:
marathon:

Have students work on these and other "word conditions" at home or in groups. It reinforces dictionary skills as well as Internet research, and can be sort of addictive for students and their parents.

Remember the earlier "corruptions," for example, vermin being pronounced "varmint"? A sixth grader discovered an eponymous corruption. The word is "bedlam," a place of noisy confusion, a mad house (think of a middle school dance or possibly a lunch period). It turns out that it's derived from the Cockney pronunciation of "Bethlehem," from the asylum Hospital of St. Mary of Bethlehem in London.

It's amazing how our language grows and grows. Eponyms are examples of additions to our language. Doing word play gets students genuinely curious about words and where they originated.

CLIPPED WORDS

Again, students find these to be fun to collect. Some teachers set aside sections of their students' writers' notebooks. Start the students off with easy examples:

exam—examination
limo—limousine
demo—demonstration
gym—gymnasium
dorm—dormitory
vet—veterinarian, veteran

Macho (from the Spanish word *machismo*) is a recent addition to the English language. Additionally, a combination of eponym and clipping, the word "tuxedo" came from Tuxedo Park Country Club, got generalized to a formal suit, *and* is now clipped and used quite often as "tux."

A few other clippings to get your students following:

ad	flu	pen
auto	fridge	prof
bike	gas	ref
champ	lunch	sub
coed	math	tech
con	mum	typo
drape	pants	ump

The children "collect" their clipped words and the longer version. What's important is the talk when they share with their peers. They discover, for example, that "sub" can refer to a substitute or submarine. They recognize that "pen" can be clipped word for penitentiary, or stands alone as a writing instrument.

WORD BLENDS (PORTMANTEAU WORDS)

These blends also kind of infiltrate our language. They are slang-like, but usually make perfect sense. As with the previous sets, give children examples; you may wish to do a word map (see figure 9.1).

Remind your student that each part usually is a *part*, not a whole word, for example, mo(tor) + ped(al) makes *moped*, not motorped, not mopedal.

brunch = breakfast + lunch	modem = modulator + demodulator
chortle = chuckle + snort	moped = motor + pedal
chump = chunk + lump	motorcade = motor + cavalcade
conman = confidence + man	napalm = nathene + palmitute
flare = flame + glare	paratroops = parachute + troops
flurry = flutter + hurry	skylab = sky + laboratory
fortnight = fourteen + nights	travelogue = travel + monologue
glimmer = gleam + shimmer	twinight = twin + night
hifi = high + fidelity	wedlock = wedding + lock

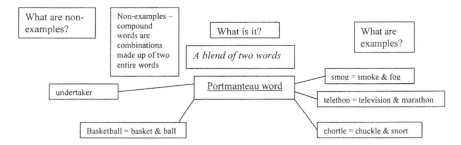

Figure 9.1. Word Map (word blends)

ACRONYMS

Acronyms are usually made up of the first letters of their component words, although sometimes letters are skipped and added. Acronyms are pronounced as one word, as in SCUBA (self-contained underwater breathing apparatus). Initialisms, such as FBI, are shortcuts where each individual letter is said, so ZIP (as in code) is an acronym, because we say "ZIP" not "Z-I-P." The problem that muddies the waters is that ASAP, for example, is both—some people say "A-S-A-P," others say "ASAP."

Following are acronym examples. Many are of military origin. Be careful of the laundered and unlaundered versions that occur, such as SNAFU meaning "situation normal, all *fouled* up."

AIDS = Acquired Immune Deficiency Syndrome
AWOL = Absent without Leave
CARE = Cooperative for American Relief Everywhere
FICA = Federal Insurance Contributions Act
MADD = Mothers against Drunk Driving
MASH = Mobile Army Surgical Hospital
NOW – National Organization for Women
OPEC = Organization of Petroleum Exporting Countries
PIN = Personal Identification Number
SONAR = Sound Navigation and Ranging
VISTA = Volunteers in Service to America

INITIALISMS

As mentioned previously, the individual letters in initialisms are uttered. Many of these have more than one "meaning"; for example, IRA stands for (at least) Irish Republican Army, Individual Retirement Account, and International Reading Association. Here are a few. This time I have not provided all of the answers. Students might be more familiar with such initialisms as TTY and OMG from texting:

ABC = American Broadcasting Corporation
AMA = American Medical Association
CPA = Certified Public Accountant
CPR = cardiopulmonary resuscitation
DOA = dead on arrival
FBI = Federal Bureau of Investigation
FDC =
HBO =
IOU =
IQ =
IRS =
KO =
MBA =
MIA =
NRA =
PHD =
RIP =
RSVP =
RV =
SOS =
SWAK =
TGIF =
TLC =
UFO =
VIP =

HOMOPHONES AND HOMOGRAPHS

Homophones are words that are spelled differently but are pronounced the same. Homographs are words that are spelled alike but are different in meaning and (sometimes) in pronunciation. Both can present persistent spelling and usage problems. Children and adults run the spell checker, but at times leave the wrong word that sounds (and is spelled) "right" but is not correct in that context. It is often effective when teachers teach homophones in sets, in order to contrast them.

Students need constant reinforcement on your/you're, who's/whose, too/
to/two, its/it's. Some homophone sets that occur less often, are listed here:

aide/aid
altar/alter
affect/effect
ascent/assent
base/bass
bough/bow
callous/callus
censor/sensor
cite/site/sight
coop/coupe
cue/queue
desert/dessert
dual/duel
flew/flu/flue
idle/idol
lead/led
manner/manor
might/mite
passed/past
pedal/peddle/petal
principal/principle
rain/rein/reign
right/rite/write
role/roll
seam/seem
stationary/stationery
taught/taut
threw/through
thyme/time
vane/vain/vein
ware/where/wear
yoke/yolk

It's a bit contrived, but encourage attempts at putting the set into one
sentence—whether it's a cloze situation of whether the students create the
sentence, for example, Gilbert *threw* the ball *through* the window. The *aide*
will *aid* the general in preparing the plan. For more on homophones, see appendix 4-B.

What's tricky is that some words that are homophones are also homographs, for example, "desert" is part of a homophone set when it is paired with "dessert" (i.e., "desert" as a verb, meaning to abandon), but "desert" is also a homograph (i.e., "desert" as the verb above, or the arid place—like the Sahara). Here are examples:

bass—a fish, rhymes with "pass"; low sound, rhymes with "pace"
bow—shoots arrows, rhymes with "no"; bend at the waist, rhymes with "now"
conduct—
contract—
converse—
does—
excuse—
lead—
minute—
perfect—
present—
primer—
record—
refuse—
sow—a female pig is called a *sow*. The gardener will *sow* her seeds in March.
subject—
tear—
use—
wind—The *wind* howled, and the shelter shook. I am going to *wind* up the
   toy mouse.

Either supply students with sentences with the words used in a rich context, or have them create the same. The use is much more likely to stick than with a definition. For more on homographs and homophones see appendices 4-A and 4-B.

SIMILES AND METAPHORS

Similes and metaphors are excellent for teaching the concept of clichés, and for eliminating trite, hackneyed language and moving toward lively comparisons that make written language richer. This little section, then, overlaps with chapter 6, which deals with vocabulary growth and use in written language.

Similes are figures of speech using the words "like" or "as," functioning like adverbs or adjectives. They modify or describe a person, place, thing, or action with a colorful and often visual phrase. Creative writers make good use of both devices. Metaphors, on the other hand, compare two things but do not use "like" or "as." Students must learn not to take them literally, but to appreciate their use. Similes and metaphors follow (note that the similes are also clichés):

Similes
as busy as a bee
as busy as a beaver
as cool as a cucumber
as cold as ice
as green as grass
as light as a feather
as quiet as a mouse
as smooth as glass
as stubborn as a mule
slept like a log
eat like a pig
work like a dog
works like a charm
cry like a baby
fits like a glove

Metaphors
Jealousy is a green-eyed monster.
He is the shining light in her life.
She needs to be handled with kid gloves.
Jerome is faster than a locomotive.
My love is a river.
She has porcelain skin.
John has a hollow leg.
I'm a real chicken when it comes to dating.

More follow in appendix 4-G.

The metaphors listed are also idioms—they are challenging for second language learners, as well as anyone else who takes language too literally. A friend visited the Czech Republic recently. While there, as he learned the language, an acquaintance questioned his use of the word "henpecked." She said that the equivalent circumstance in her language was termed "under the slipper"!

When doing similes and metaphors as an activity with students, first try to elicit the conventional by doing these as fill-in-the-blank items. You may

choose to cover the creative column, doing the conventional column as a class
or conventional group. Then talk to your students about clichés, then move
on to the creative column.

	Conventional	*Creative*
as cold as	_____	*an assassin's heart*
fits like a	_____	*size 8 dress on a size 12 woman*
works like a	_____	*grad student on exam week*
cry like a	_____	_____
as light as a	_____	_____
as stubborn as	_____	_____
as nervous as	_____	_____
slept like a	_____	_____
as hard as	_____	_____
as hungry as a	_____	*salesperson on commission*

Try to teach your students to be divergent and flexible in their connotations
of conventional words like hard, cry, cold, light—they can then break away
from conventional images. For more on similes and metaphors see appendices 4-F and 4-G. You'll also quite possibly enjoy appendix 5-D, containing
bad analogies that actually appeared in student writing.

OXYMORONS

Students enjoy these contradictions of terms: jumbo shrimp, working vacation, gourmet hotdogs, military intelligence, friendly fire. These can be
brainstormed in pairs, whole class, or in some other combination. The activity
can be a game, or it can involve a homework assignment. Here's a double
oxymoron that a student came up with: fresh frozen jumbo shrimp.

ALLITERATION

Musical lyrics and poetry are great sources of alliteration, the repetition of
initial sounds. The lyrics of popular music can really get students' attention,
but be careful of infringing upon copyrights. Let's say you are doing a unit on
the 1960s, and the students are reading about events at Kent State University.
You play a song by a foursome with the first names of Neil, Steven, David,
and Graham. Then you make a connection to alliteration, using an alliterative
string using the word "lilting."

Now, words are free in isolation, but how far do I have to go before I infringe on the musicians' territory? Lilting lady? Lacy lilting? Same thing with assonance; hypnotizing won't cost me five thousand dollars in permission fees. Mesmerizing won't either, but if put those two words together, it may be expensive.

PSEUDONYMS

Pseudonyms, literally "false names," are also called stage names or pen names. In introducing these to students, it is easiest to start with examples and have the students discover the "definition." Below are a few examples of some famous pseudnonymous names. Pseudonyms are not quite the same as aliases, but to differentiate the two categories would be a very interesting activity. These are fun for students to research and talk about; you may branch off into foreign phrases (nom de plume) when you do these.

Samuel L. Clemens =
Theodore Geisel =
Robert Zimmerman =
Francis Gumm =
Erik Weiss =
Archibald Leach =
Lew Alcindor =

WORD PLAY/RIDDLES

Here the teacher generates a few to start, then turns it over to the students. This is not vocabulary instruction per se, and it is not the way to teach those rarer words. But children must think flexibly, and some good incidental teaching can occur.

26 = 1 _ _ _ _ _ _ of the a _ _ _ _ _ _ _ (letters, alphabet)
5 = d _ _ _ _ _ in a z _ _ c _ _ _ (digits, zip code)
7 = c_ _ _ _ _ _ _ _ _ in the w _ _ _ _ (continents, world)
13 = s _ _ _ _ _ _ on the A _ _ _ _ _ _ _ f _ _ _

More number riddles appear in appendix 2-C.

Here are some riddles using the names of NFL teams:

overexposed sunbathers = Redskins
maritime birds = Seahawks
a dollar per piece of corn = Buccaneers (buck an ear)
refrigerator invaders = Raiders
Nixon's wife goes berserk = Patriots (Pat + riots)
your father's sisters in the army = Giants (G.I. + aunts)
girl's toy's appendages = Dolphins (doll + fins)
credit card users = Chargers

For more of these riddles, see appendix 2-A. Please note that the NFL teams as riddles are based on old handouts used with ninth graders some years ago. Updates were necessary because the league expands and some franchises move.

CAPITONYMS

These are words that are very much like homographs (e.g., bass and bass, lead and lead, desert and desert), but when one is capitalized it changes both pronunciation and meaning:

Polish—polish
Nice—nice
Job—job

These are pretty challenging. Reserve them for older and more capable students, and spend a few minutes brainstorming with the entire class.

ILLUSTRATED WORDS AND PHRASES

The object is to represent a familiar phrase or cliché. Some easy examples follow:

arrest   ⮕   you're under arrest
you're

injury + insult   ⮕   adding insult to injury

belt hitting	⮞	hitting below the belt
V I O L E T s	⮞	shrinking violets
C C GARAGE R R	⮞	two car garage
house prairie	⮞	little house on the prairie
sleeping job	⮞	sleeping on the job
eggs easy	⮞	eggs over easy
P A I N S	⮞	growing pains
MAN campus	⮞	big man on campus

Middle school students truly enjoy getting creative. They simply need your permission.

SYNONYM SWAPPING

Here are some word pairs. In each "set," try to take away one letter from one word and add the *same letter* to the other word to make synonyms. For example, *simulate* and *spurt*: you take the *t* away from *spurt* to make the word *spur*; *spur* is a synonym for *stimulate*, which was formed by adding the *t* that was taken away from spurt. One more example: *trough* and *study*: take the *r* from *trough*, and get *tough* and *sturdy*.

1. weary, carful
2. grove, rout
3. contract, each
4. singe, lone
5. bawl, fright

6. treason, though
7. boar, salon
8. dam, wept
9. budget, sir
10. peasant, flair

ONOMATOPOEIA

These words are borrowed from sounds, in that they resemble or imitate the sounds of the words. They are favorites of cartoon strip writers and poets. Here are some examples:

beep	chirp	crash	giggle	moo	slurp	squish
buzz	clank	crunch	growl	quack	sputter	zip

SNIGLETS AND NEW WORDS (NEOLOGISMS)

These were popular twenty years ago, as tags for invented words. They are loads of fun and really get children thinking out of the box.

As of the drafting of this manuscript, the American Dialectic Association, which, for example, voted "truthiness" the word of the year in 2005, was considering some of the items below for word of the year in 2008:

cheedle (n) the residue left under one's finger nails, orange in color, after eating cheese doodles

nuptcrastination (n) staying a bachelor as long as possible

amorlapse (v) running into your other significant other

polygynastics (n) dating several women at the same time

hyperinclining (v) all the way back in your car seat

aquadextrous (adj) able to turn the faucets in your tub with your toes

delucidation (n) turn off the lights at night

Obamanation (n) Pallination

bailout (n)

maverick/mavericking (n) Pallination

going rogue (v)

obamamania (n)

recessionista/frugalista (n) living well despite a bad economy

credit crunch (n) we are living in one

bread crumbs (n) the digital record of where you (and perhaps Gretel) have been in cyberspace

swagga (n) a donation from the hip-hop world

OPM (n) other people's money

More Neologisms

These are adult/workplace examples, but they can certainly serve as models for children.

stress puppy: person who seems to thrive on being stressed out and whiny
irritainment: entertainment and media spectacles that are annoying but you
find yourself unable to stop watching them
percussive maintenance: the fine art of whacking the tar out of an electronic
generica: features of the American landscape that are exactly the same no
matter where one is, such as fast food joints, strip malls, subdivisions
cube farm: an office filled with cubicles
prairie dogging: when someone yells or drops something loudly in a cube
farm, and people's heads pop up over the walls to see what's going on
mouse potato: online, wired generation's answer to the couch potato
sitcoms: Single Income, Two Children, Oppressive Mortgage; what yuppies
turn into when they have children and one of them stops working to stay
home with the kids

TELL ME HOW

In this activity, the teacher names a verb and the students must think of some
adverbs that go with the word. For example, teacher picks "laughed" and
children say "loudly" and "lustily" (you just got a good start on a lesson on
alliteration).

In the examples that follow, the teacher may limit the adverbs to one or two
per item, and might stipulate that no adverbs may be repeated—this requires
the students to really think. Have a recorder keep track.

whistled _____
laughed _____
floated _____
stared _____
leaned _____
danced _____
watched _____
sat _____
paced _____
drove _____
disappeared _____
yelled _____
stopped _____
played _____
tiptoed _____
dropped _____
purrs _____
slept *soundly, deeply*

TWO-WAY WORDS

The following words are both nouns and verbs. Based on the context you create, you can make the words function as you please. Feel free to add endings and change word forms.

hide: I'm going to tan your *hide* (n). Bill is *hiding* in the corner (v).
paste:
look:
doubt:
vote:
cut:
stack:
cough:
permit:
play:
duck:
face:
tip:
pump:
dial:

ONE-LETTER MAGIC

Add one letter to make a new word. You may not add an s or an e at the end of the word; for example, if the word is "rat" you may not change it to "rats" or "rate."

stars—starts	bear—	bars—
power—powder	hill—	bat—
heap—	hen—	sell—
chef—	lead—	plan—
mile—	pond—	hose—

PARONOMASIA (TO PLAY ON WORDS)

These were sent from that electronic superhighway in the sky. Again, they're amusing—but difficult to cite. The attachment came from Maureen, a graduate assistant, who got it from her father, who got it from a coworker, who got it from a friend . . . but there the trail ran cold.

1. Two vultures board an airplane, each carrying two dead raccoons. The stewardess looks at them and says, "I'm sorry, gentlemen, only one carrion allowed per passenger."
2. Two boll weevils grew up in South Carolina. One went to Hollywood and became a famous actor. The other stayed behind in the cotton fields and never amounted to much. The second one, naturally, became known as the lesser of two weevils.
3. A three-legged dog walks into a saloon in the Old West. He sidles up to the bar and announces, "I'm looking for the man who shot my paw."
4. Mahatma Gandhi, as you know, walked barefoot most of the time, which produced an impressive set of calluses on his feet. He also ate very little, which made him rather frail and with his odd diet, he suffered from bad breath. This made him . . . a super calloused fragile mystic hexed by halitosis.
5. And finally, there was a girl who sent ten different puns to friends, with the hope that at least one of the puns would make them laugh. Unfortunately, no pun in ten did.

MORE PLAY

How about some thematic "barbarianisms?" It's sort of a hinky pinky offshoot. So you start off with a quick little story about "Conan the Barbarian," then introduce some sample riddles:

Q: What do you call a philanthropic Conan?
A: Conan the Humanitarian

Q: What do you call an eighty-year-old Conan?
A: Conan the Octogenarian

Q: What do you call a non-meat-eating Conan?
A: Conan the Vegetarian

Q: What do you call Conan born in the ninth sign of the Zodiac?
A: Conan the Saggitarian

Q: What do you call a fair-minded Conan?
A: Conan the Egalitarian

Q: What do you call Conan born in the eleventh sign of the Zodiac?
A: Conan the Aquarian

Q: What do you call a book-oriented Conan?
A: Conan the Librarian

Q: What do you call Conan at a liberal church?
A: Conan the Unitarian

Q: What do you call a farming Conan?
A: Conan the Agrarian

Q: What do you call Conan from the first state?
A: Conan the Delawarian

Q: What do you call Conan teaching English?
A: Conan the Grammarian

These are pretty silly. But they can be great fun as well.

QUICKSTORMS

Have your students quickly write words that fit into certain parameters, for example words that start with the letter s and end in –ion: How about p and -ate?

station	starvation	private	primate
satiation	secretion	profligate	procrastinate
solution	salutation	plate	
suspicion	seduction	predate	

IMPONDERABLES

These are amusing slogans and questions. Middle school students have a great time with them!

Why is the man who invests all of your money called a broker?
If cats like to eat mice so much, why don't they have mouse-flavored cat food?

If ignorance is bliss, why aren't more people happy?

When cheese gets its picture taken, what does it say?

If the black box flight recorder is never damaged during a plane accident, why don't we make the whole plane out of the stuff?

What if the hokey pokey is what it's all about?

If a word is misspelled in the dictionary, how would we ever know?

Why do we sing "Take me out to the ball game" when we are already there?

Why are a "wise man" and a "wise guy" opposites?

Why is "phonics" not spelled the way it sounds?

How come "abbreviated" is such a long word?

Why is it that doctors call what they do "practice"?

Why is the time of day with the slowest traffic called rush hour?

If con is the opposite of pro, is Congress the opposite of progress?

If flying is so safe, why do they call the airport the terminal?

Why is the alphabet in that order, is it because of that song?

CONCLUDING REMARKS

Word play can be a lot of pun, errr, fun! Be sure to mix seriousness of purpose with a little levity; your students will thank you. Adults need a little variety and a smattering of laughter, and so do children. It may not be scientifically based, but the slots on that hard to reach child's schema just may be more easily accessed via humor!

Chapter Ten

The Assessment of Vocabulary, Including Test Preparation

Not everything that matters can be counted; not everything that can be counted, matters.

—Albert Einstein

TEST PREP

It's time for the state tests in three weeks, and principal Barry Schwab is concerned about the vocabulary scores of the third, fourth, and fifth graders in his elementary building. He has purchased test prep materials at considerable expense, and he has determined that all *teachers in grades 3, 4, and 5 will use the purchased materials for an hour a day, every day for the three weeks prior to the high-stakes testing.*

Elaine Moore is a fourth grade teacher in the building in question. She also is a member of the school literacy committee, as well as a similar district-wide committee. Elaine is conversant with the research about vocabulary instruction, and she has gone on record as being opposed to the purchase of the materials (many trade books could have been purchased instead, as well as sets of leveled books!) and the mandate that they be used in a cramming fashion just prior to the tests. Elaine understands the "no quick fix" truth: she recognizes that the test-prep materials are keyed to and mirror the state test, and she realizes that familiarity in the format will result in some possible cosmetic gains—but she feels that children will not in fact have better vocabulary knowledge in the long run as a result of the cramming.

*Elaine broaches her concern to her principal. She offers to work with
the intermediate teachers in order to familiarize them with best practice
that can be embedded in literacy instruction throughout the year. Principal Schwab refuses her offer, and tells her to stick with the program.*

Tests, ostensibly, are given in order to garner information that is useful to
someone. At times, large-scale tests are given to evaluate programs or innovations. There is a burgeoning trend to measure teacher effectiveness, as well,
through standardized assessments conducted by districts, states, and even the
federal government. At the classroom level, teachers observe their students
in action, examine their work, give tests and quizzes, and decide where their
students need help.

The classroom instructional designs are important; the standardized data
result in important resource allocation decisions—and many dollars are spent
largely based on testing data. In district after district, comparisons are made,
and for every winner there's an equal and opposite loser. We spend too much
time measuring and testing! Additionally, this trend is extremely expensive,
in terms of time and money.

Vocabulary assessment can be generally classified as either *formative* or
summative. Formative assessments are classroom based, look like good instruction, and *inform* instruction. Summative assessments are "external"—the
high-stakes state and national tests that are on most teachers' minds so much
these days. We shall begin with some discussion of summative (either criterion-referenced or norm-referenced) tests.

ASSESSING VOCABULARY
SUMMATIVELY: SOME PROBLEMS

The first problem is a generalizability one related to sampling: How do we
decide which words to test? Where do the words come from? What's a sixth
grade–level word as opposed to a fifth- or a seventh-grade word? If you're
reading a work such as a short story, you can limit the words for your assessment to those from the selection; if, however, you're designing a standardized
measure, you have some narrowing to do. Based on the earlier three thousand
words a year estimate, an eighth grader will have learned eighteen thousand
new words (3,000 x 6) since leaving the primary grades. How do we decide
the important words to test?

Second, what does it mean to "know" a word? Is pronouncing it enough?
How about generating its definition? Which definition? As opposed to

generating, how about choosing the best answer? The issue is a tough one: it involves constructed responses versus selected responses. What about being able to *use* it appropriately, either orally or in writing—or both? How about being able to provide examples of it, or synonyms, or name its function? How about some combination of the above? How about all of the above? A final issue has to do with knowledge of a word "situation." In whatever format you choose, students may forget a word or may not recognize it.

Third, in what format do we "test" our selection of words from among the 2 million? How do we "test content"? Plugging the words into analogies? With sentence completion? Choosing synonyms or generating synonyms? Antonyms? Some of the above ways? All of the above? In order to ascertain whether a child "knows" a word, we can try many formats: Johnson and Pearson (1978) examined vocabulary test formats and found that children who "knew" a word one way did not, often, know the same word when it was tested a different way.

TESTING REALITIES

All of the states have required testing programs in place—at least in reading and math. Some states use published standardized tests, while others have developed their own assessments. Schools are sorted and ranked using these tests, and the results are usually published. People move into districts and buy houses in certain school boundary areas based on these scores. In some states the assessments are truly "high stakes" because schools that perform poorly may be sanctioned in a variety of ways, and some individuals may (for example) not graduate. Financial carrots may be dangled, and the rhetoric is for "continuous improvement."

It should be remembered that there are two types of high-stakes tests. The first type is the criterion-referenced test that determines whether the students meet some predetermined standard (interestingly, and ironically, termed "cut scores"). Second, we have norm-referenced tests that compare performance with the scores of other students nationally along an assumedly bell-shaped curve.

Cut scores influence test results significantly, for they can be set arbitrarily, but norm-referenced tests ensure that there is no Lake Woebegon effect—all children cannot be above average; in fact half must be below average. It will be interesting to see how the No Child Left Behind mandate plays out in the years ahead!

SOME MEASUREMENT DIFFICULTIES

Following is a discussion of testing in general. We'll then focus on specific vocabulary tests.

Validity

Content validity rests on the foundation of opinions of experts who have been asked to judge whether the items measure what they purport to. The essential question is this: does the test really measure what it says it does? Tests that are high in validity often lack reliability; similarly, very reliable tests (and test items) often have limited validity.

Reliability

Test makers love reliability—essentially, how well a test agrees with itself, and how consistently it will yield the same results for the same child. Reliability is usually measured as a reliability coefficient. It should be remembered that a highly reliable test may be low in validity—word learning is inherently messy—and if it's *valid*, then it's entirely possible that it may not be terribly reliable. The Einstein quote at the beginning of this chapter was chosen for a reason!

Objectivity

A test is objective if it is "fair," for example, if some children get more time than others to complete a section, it's not objective. Or if some test takers get to use dictionaries and some do not, results will clearly be contaminated. Testing conditions need to be similar; the playing field should be level. If children's home lives were also "equitable," we might be able to draw some conclusions from these tests regarding efficacy of instruction.

Norming

For comparison purposes, norming is done through sampling procedures. The sample is selected, scores are translated into grade level equivalents or percentile ranks, and these scores are the "standard" against which future test takers are scored.

Other Issues

There are several other concerns, among them the content of these tests is often outdated; there are cultural and linguistic biases; and, the tests lack diagnostic value. Tests, in and of themselves, are not "bad" things. We should remember that it's not the test results that may stigmatize children; it's the things that are *done with* the results!

Let's now take a more specific look at standardized group vocabulary tests. Most standardized reading tests yield a composite score made up of vocabulary and comprehension subtests. Of course, given what we know about the "loading" of vocabulary ability on comprehension, there should be pretty great agreement between the two. At any rate, the format usually involves a multiple-choice selection of a synonym for the target word.

> From the group below *choose* the *one* word with the closest meaning to *maroon*
>   a) pasta
>   b) dessert
>   c) shoal
>   d) dark red

For a majority of tests, the vocabulary words selected are drawn from high-frequency graded word lists from "grade level" science and social studies texts as well as from reading anthologies (Cooter, 1990). Even though there exists the previously mentioned high correlation between vocabulary and comprehension, these tests can provide a *rough* estimate of a students' prior knowledge as well as their ability to make broad associations to new words.

Here's another issue that needs to be considered. Vocabulary tests measure the most superficial aspects of word learning. Selecting a synonym in no way equates to the ability to use a word flexibly and richly. As the sample test item presented earlier was created, the test item maker limited himself to the first word he saw on the page that was randomly selected: it was "maroon." He used "maroon" in the color mode because "to leave (a person) alone in an uninhabited place" is too long a definition, and the distracters (i.e., the other choices) would need to be of appropriately equal length.

Remember, too, that vocabulary tests are measures of decoding—poor decoders may "miss" items, even when the words are in their oral vocabularies. Additionally, if the words are presented in context, the scores might be quite different as opposed to the words being presented in isolation. We must remember that choosing a word to match another in a list of words is very unlike actual reading tasks.

Several years ago a sixth grade student named Corrine was a struggling reader who was placed in a fast track because she was good in math (go figure). Her teacher was required to cover vocabulary as prescribed by the gurus in some far-off place.

Corrine was doing a multiple-choice item with the targeted word "irascible" (she pronounced with a hard C "iraskible"). When the teacher asked her about the other three words, she didn't have a clue about those, either. Yet when the teacher looked at Corrine's bubbled-in answers, he found they were all correct. He asked Corrine how she arrived at her answers. She said she didn't read the sentences; she just skimmed the four choices for the "hardest" or "longest" and always chose that one. If he had not asked her and had simply looked at her answer choices, he would have assumed she knew all the words.

VOCABULARY TEST PREPARATION

How well does the curriculum match the test, and how does the teacher help students prepare for such tests? It is wise to think of reading tests as another genre of reading, to be taught as such. Short of teaching the actual words (which would be cheating), teachers can provide practice with the common vocabulary test formats. There is certainly no substitute for knowing a lot of words richly and deeply—but basic knowledge being about equal, it is very useful to be familiar with the testing formats.

As an example, if the test you're required to administer to fourth graders contains analogies, it is pretty unfair not to provide your students with some explicit instruction on analogies. To do so does not mean that you abandon good teaching or that you're cheating. Teach children to be flexible, using a think-aloud model!

In order to ascertain how well students have absorbed, say, a fifth grade list of three hundred vocabulary words, we can quiz them on thirty items from the list in order to reach a conclusion. James Popham (2004) simply urges that educators differentiate between *item teaching* and *curriculum teaching*. As long as teachers don't teach directly toward a set of items on a particular test, it is probable that their curriculum teaching helps students to acquire skills in a variety of in-school and outside settings. For example, good teaching of Latin and Greek word parts, generally, will result in students being able to figure out many new words.

Good teachers (whose students "happen" to score high) stress vocabulary development and provide continual opportunities for vocabulary growth in both oral and written language—and they do so all year long, not just the two weeks before the testing event. Additionally, they teach their children how to use vocabulary learning strategies and they engage their students in game-like language play activities. Finally, they encourage and "expect" and nudge and create cultures where utilization of all types of written materials takes place.

SPECIALIZED VOCABULARY TESTS

High-stakes tests, whether norm referenced or criterion referenced, are broad measures that provide programmatic information. For more diagnostic information related to individual student performance, it is preferable to use the formative, "organic" assessments that teachers can use in the daily pulse of the classroom. However, to corroborate and validate that information, some specialized tests may at times be warranted.

Special Needs Diagnosis

Informal Reading Inventories (IRI) are individual assessments. They are classified as "informal" diagnostic measures, but they can be quite rigorous. They can be commercially constructed, or may be developed by teachers. They consist of word lists at various levels, which are used to "enter" a child at the appropriate passages for oral and silent reading. Due to the individual nature of this test, the examiner can delve and probe and learn about the student's reasoning processes.

Closely related to the IRI is the running record. In this assessment, teachers use IRI-like conventions to mark either a photocopy of the text or a blank sheet of paper. The running record is a form of miscue analysis, conceptually holding to the notion that departures from text are not always errors, but rather windows into a reader's strategies. Running records can be used to figure accuracy levels for placement in texts, but are most useful for determining "teaching points."

Formative Assessments

Formative assessments are rooted in the classroom. They are the answers to the type of questions that teachers ask in order to inform instruction. Teachers want to know if the things they are doing are working, and formative assessment can help determine proper avenues to pursue.

Teachers need to gather a range of data, using an array of instructional methods and looking for patterns in order to determine how their students are doing. Standardized group measures are a rough start, but they cannot inform the way careful watching and diagnostic teaching can. Additionally, such information must be collected, stored, analyzed, and retrieved expeditiously.

Pre- and Post-Graphic Organizers

In chapters 4 and 5 a broad array of graphic organizers were presented: maps, webs, the Frayer Model, semantic feature analysis, and the like. By looking at these measures before and after reading, the teacher can ascertain what a student *knew* in terms of vocabulary, and what she presently *knows*. This type of assessment allows the teacher to keep tabs on word learning without obtrusive testing of vocabulary, and helps to plan for further instruction. Following are some ideas for assessing vocabulary that are congruent with good instruction.

Word Maps

The various word maps presented in earlier chapters allow the teacher to understand how completely, how deeply, students understand certain terms. Occasional probes, again before and after instruction, are useful in order for teachers to determine if their instruction has been indeed absorbed. Following is a vignette wrapped around a concept map (figure 10.1) that is used before and after a unit.

FORMATIVE ASSESSMENT

Theresa Butym teaches fifth grade in a self-contained elementary school. Her students have done a lot of webbing and are used to the format. Theresa is about to launch into a unit on the rain forest, and is providing her students with a partial map (see figure 10.1).

She tells her students that they are to fill in the four "fingers" in each of the categories, just to see what they already know; they may use only one word for each finger.

At the end of the unit she gives them the same map.

Three-Minute Meetings

A teacher selects ten words from a child's notebook collection, word bank, or other source and asks students to use them in a meaningful way. Using a checklist format, the teacher can record performances over time. These are quick and useful, truly user friendly for teachers and students alike.

Yea/Nay

This is a game-like activity (Beck & McKeown, 2003) that can be used for a quick assessment. It requires some teacher preparation in the beginning, but control can be turned over to the students. It can be done with small or large

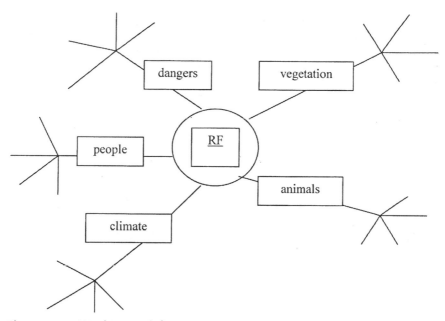

Figure 10.1.   Word Map (rainforest)

groups. Students have two cards, one saying "yes" and the other saying "no." Teachers ask questions such as the following:

Would a person who is *obstinate* be argumentative?
Would a speaker who *gesticulates* "talk with his hands"?
Would it help a gymnast to be *nimble*?
Would it help a power lifter to be *nimble*?
Might a conceited person *swagger* when he walks?

After each question, the teacher gives some wait time, counts to three, and the students simultaneously hold up their cards to indicate agreement or disagreement. As with many good formative assessments, this can be a useful teaching tool—the teacher can get inside kids' heads by inviting explanation and/or revision of sentences to change the response. Once a student learns how to create her own sentences, they can be banked for future use.

Teacher-Constructed Tests

Teacher-made tests and quizzes can take a variety of forms. Again, teachers like it when children are empowered to create and "donate" test items as well as the target words themselves. This really helps children to get inside of the test construction enterprise.

A key here is a variety of formats. To be fair to your students, you should probably teach test language and formats that they may encounter. For example, generative responses are preferable to "bubble-in" formats. Vocabulary assessments, when not oral, are usually generative—that is, congruent with best practice in instruction. But also teach students multiple choice as a weird genre of assessment, thinking aloud as the teacher acts like a test maker. After you create a test item or two, have students do the same.

STUDENT SELF-EVALUATION

Someone has said, "If you want to appear accountable, test your students . . . but if you want to be truly accountable for student learning, teach them to self-assess." It is imperative that students not be dependent upon the teacher as sole arbiter of what constitutes "quality." Along with teacher-controlled introspective methods, self-evaluation by students is a critical component in developing balance in word learning. In fact, self-assessment is a very transportable skill. Additionally, structures such as literature circles often use role sheets for vocabulary directors (aka "word wizards"), which also serves to elevate the function.

Another possibility involves whatever format the teacher prefers for word collection, such as journals or the vocabulary section of the writer's notebook. The teacher might also formalize the self-reflection process by including it periodically, to pull together sections of student work. The following excerpt is from Jason's writer's notebook.

JASON

This quarter I read four SSR books, in addition to the readings that were assigned to me. I collected eighty words using the bookmark method, twenty from each of the books. I shared a lot of those words with my cooperative group. I like all of my picks, but there are two words I am especially proud of: "tawdry" and "Mayday." Dr. G. came in and taught us some cool stuff about where words came from, and one of the things I like was what he called "corruptions," or alterations words that get mispronounced and stay that way, like vittles for victuals.

When I found tawdry, which means showy in a cheap way, the dictionary called it an "alternation" of St. Audrey which developed into 'tawdry and eventually "tawdry." I thought that was interesting. As far as Mayday goes, I knew before that it's kind of like "SOS, SOS! Mayday, Mayday!" It's something that's called out when a ship is in trouble. I found out that it is also an alternation, this time from French (which I am studying this year)—aidez is a French verb for help and m'aidez literally means me-help, we'd translate it as "help me, I need help." I liked that one, too. There are many more stories behind most of the other seventy-eight in my word bank, but I thought you'd like these two.

Jason obviously is a pretty self-aware word learner. He is firmly in control of his own learning. He is eager to be a partner in assessing his vocabulary growth and effort, which is our segue to the final major section of this chapter, concerning record keeping.

KEEPING VOCABULARY RECORDS

Voluminous data gathering is of little use if it cannot be accessed easily and *used* to shape and drive instruction. Both students and teachers can be responsible for keeping records in the classroom that document change and growth. Here are some suggestions.

Student Ownership

Word Cards

Students can keep cumulative records of words encountered and learned. Cards can be formatted for consistency. It is preferable that words be "presented" in context, and that the vocabulary be reused in games like Shazam! (see chapter 2) or on the word wall. Some teachers have the students keep these on rings; boxes (like little recipe boxes) work well too.

Word Notebooks

Some teachers are very particular about word notebooks. Loose-leaf types are most flexible, so that words can be easily located, alphabetized, or otherwise manipulated. Smaller loose-leaf types are the best, for ease of handling, particularly if the word section is embedded in the writer's notebook.

Portfolio Self-Evaluation

Portfolios are much more than repositories for student "stuff"; they are meaningful, purposeful collections of student work. Reflection leads to goal setting, and the cycle continues: collect—select—reflect. Words learned—and in particular, self-assessment as to how words were best learned—are of critical importance.

Teacher Record Keeping

We all remember those black, shiny, ominous grade books that teachers played close to their vests. They collapsed complex learning products and process into single letters and numbers, and then summarized a child's work in a single number or letter, for the quarter, for the year. Strong teachers of vocabulary can do so much more! Teaching decisions are closely allied and informed by data collection.

Checklists

Teachers need to focus on a few students at a time, so checklists are sampling devices—but they can be quite informative. For example, the earlier "yea/nay" strategy or the "Three-Minute Meeting" results can be recorded in checklist formats.

Anecdotal Records

Another form of ongoing record keeping is the anecdotal record. Again, teachers need to limit themselves in terms of breadth and go for depth by focusing on a limited number of children at a time. Teachers use everything from file cards to Post-it notes to address labels.

Assessment goes far beyond high-stakes testing formats. Measurement-driven instruction distorts the learning possibilities if teachers shift the focus away from teaching students to read well and instead teaching only the skills needed to perform well on the test (Popham, 2004). Depending on a teacher's *purpose*, she should be able to choose from a wide array of assessment devices/formats. From student self-assessment to teacher-made tests to standardized information, these snapshots can be organized into useful newsreels.

Appendices

ADDITIONAL RESOURCES

ACTIVITIES

OUR LANGUAGE KEEPS GROWING

USEFUL LISTS

THEY SAID IT

Additional Resources

Busy teachers find the information highway to be a great source—but they rarely have time to evaluate sites carefully. Additionally, it is actually difficult to stay up to date.

www.crazythoughts.com
Source of some of the imponderables in chapter 9

www.indiana.edu/~eric_rec/ieo/digests/d126.html
ERIC Digest: Vocabulary and Reading Comprehension
Prepared by ERIC Clearinghouse on Reading, English, and Communication; discusses the importance vocabulary plays in reading comprehension

www.puzzledepot.com/
Challenges your brain with free puzzles, Shockwave and Flash games, crosswords, logic games, IQ tests, trivia games, and contests for prizes

www.quia.com/
Allows teachers to create their own activities, puzzles, games, or quizzes online or to access hundreds of activities created by other educators in all content areas

www.teachingmadeeasier.com
Commercial site

www.abcteach.com
Over five thousand free printable pages and worksheets plus crossword puzzles and word searches

www.readinga-z.com
Downloadable materials to teach guided reading, phonics, and the alphabet, including lessons plans

www.teachers.net
Over a hundred teacher chat boards and loads of lesson plans; a great way to exchange ideas and strategies

www.proteacher.net
Thirty-six discussion boards and opportunities for teachers to share (and be paid) as writers

www.wordplays.com
Anagrams, crossword puzzles, boggles, word morphs, crypto cracker

www.rhymezone.com
Devoted to online rhyming possibilities; type in a word to find rhymes, synonyms, definitions

dictionary.cambridge.org
Free online English dictionaries, phrase collections, idioms, and so on

www.vocabulary.com
Three levels of difficulty: test preparation, crossword puzzles, synonyms, and antonyms

www.yourdictionary.com
Links to more than two thousand dictionaries in more than 260 languages

www.bartleby.com
Contains the published works of a limited number of authors

www.m-w.com/dictionary.htm
Website title is Merriam-Webster Online: The Language Center

wordcentral.com
Operated by Merriam-Webster and designed for children

www.readwritethink.org
Website produced by the International Reading Association and the National Council of Teachers of English

www.eduplace.com/rdg/hmsv
Exhaustive, thorough; authored by luminaries Shane Templeton and Donald Bear for Houghton Mifflin.

www.vobulary.co.il
Loads of vocabulary games, puzzles, and other fun stuff.

www.funbrain.com/words.html
Inviting, enticing; components for children, parents, and teachers.

www.surfnetkids.com/vocabulary.htm
Vocabulary activities and much, much more . . . perfect for the wired generation.

Activities

APPENDIX 2-A: STRATEGIES FOR SOLVING ANALOGIES

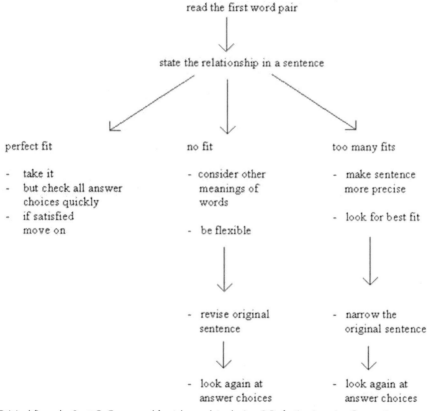

read the first word pair

state the relationship in a sentence

perfect fit

- take it
- but check all answer choices quickly
- if satisfied move on

no fit

- consider other meanings of words

- be flexible

- revise original sentence

- look again at answer choices

too many fits

- make sentence more precise

- look for best fit

- narrow the original sentence

- look again at answer choices

Original figure by Scott C. Greenwood for Advanced Analogies; © Perfection Learning Corporation. Used with Permission.

APPENDIX 2-B: NFL TEAMS (CHAPTER 9)

Listed below are thirty-two clues to the thirty-two teams in the NFL. (Team names, not city names.) Try and guess all thirty-two correctly. *Do not* look at a list of teams.

1. protected species _____ (Eagles)
2. equestrian stunt persons _____ (Cowboys)
3. your father's military sisters _____ (Giants) *(G.I. + aunts)*
4. red birds _____ (Cardinals)
5. one dollar for corn _____ (Buccaneers)
6. six rulers _____ (Vikings)
7. shows the facts _____ (Bears)
8. meat handlers _____ (Packers)
9. Peter and Paul _____ (Saints)
10. overexposed sunbathers _____ (Redskins)
11. ewe's mates _____ (Rams)
12. gold diggers _____ (49ers)
13. medieval fowls _____ (Falcons)
14. non-prop planes _____ (Jets)
15. charges _____ (Bills)
16. Nixon's wife goes wild _____ (Patriots)
17. girl's toy with fish appendages _____ (Dolphins)
18. young horses _____ (Colts)
19. Indian heads _____ (Chiefs)
20. maritime birds _____ (Seahawks)
21. midnight snackers _____ (Raiders)
22. credit users _____ (Chargers)
23. driller for Texas "tea" _____ (Oilers)
24. Indian cats _____ (Bengals)
25. tanned sunbathers _____ (Browns)
26. thieves _____ (Steelers)
27. kings of the jungle _____ (Lions)
28. unbroken stallions _____ (Broncos)
29. black birds _____ (Ravens)
30. mythical giants _____ (Titans)
31. black cats _____ (Panthers)
32. spotted cats _____ (Jaguars)

APPENDIX 2-C: FIND THE COUNTRY

The name of a country is hidden in each sentence below. To find it, look at the letters carefully from left to right.

1. Judy always carries her lunch in a brown bag.
2. "Before the clay begins to harden, mark your initials on your work," cautioned the art teacher.
3. At the game I met Stanley, Ruth, Eleanor, Wayne, and Carl.
4. Air and water are necessary for plants.
5. He made a mistake in dialing and reached the wrong number.
6. "Carry that box if you can, Adam," said Mother.
7. During the winter we often have sleet, hail, and snow.

China
Denmark
Norway
Iran
India
Canada
Hungary
Thailand

APPENDIX 2-D: NUMBER RIDDLES (CHAPTER 9)

In the many years since this "test" was developed, few people have been able to solve more than half of the questions on the first try. Many people report that answers occur to them long after the test has been set aside, particularly at unexpected times when their minds are relaxed. A relatively small number of individuals are able to solve the entire list of riddles.

Example:
12 = months in a year

26 = l_ _ _ _ _ _ of the a _ _ _ _ _ _ _
7 = w _ _ _ _ _ _ of the w _ _ _ _
12 = s _ _ _ _ of the z _ _ _ _ _
52 = c _ _ _ _ in a d _ _ _
88 = p _ _ _ _ k _ _ _
13 = s _ _ _ _ _ _ on the A _ _ _ _ _ _ _ f _ _ _

32 = d _ _ _ _ _ _ F _ _ _ _ _ _ _ _ _ _ at which w _ _ _ _ f _ _ _ _ _ _
18 = h _ _ _ _ on a g _ _ _ c _ _ _ _ _
90 = d _ _ _ _ _ _ in a r _ _ _ _ a _ _ _ _
200 = d _ _ _ _ _ _ for p _ _ _ _ _ _ g _ in M _ _ _ _ _ _ _
8 = s _ _ _ _ on a s _ _ _ s _ _ _
4 = q _ _ _ _ _ in a g _ _ _ _ _
24 = h _ _ _ _ in a d _ _
1 = w _ _ _ _ on a u _ _ _ _ _ _ _
5 = d _ _ _ _ _ in a z _ _ c _ _ _
57 = H _ _ _ _ v _ _ _ _ _ _ _ _ _
11 = p _ _ _ _ _ _ on an A _ _ _ _ _ _ _ _ f _ _ _ _ _ _ _ _ t _ _ _
1,000 = w _ _ _ _ that a p _ _ _ _ _ _ _ is w _ _ _ _
29 = d _ _ _ in F _ _ _ _ _ _ _ in a l _ _ _ y _ _ _
64 = s _ _ _ _ _ _ on a c _ _ _ _ _ _ _ _ _ _ _
3 = b _ _ _ _ m _ _ _ (s _ _ h _ _ t _ _ _ r _ _)

Answers:
26 = letters of the alphabet
7 = wonders of the world
12 = signs of the zodiac
52 = cards in a deck
88 = piano keys
13 = stripes on the American flag
32 = degrees Fahrenheit at which water freezes
18 = holes of a golf course
90 = degrees in a right angle
200 = dollars for a passing go in Monopoly
8 = sides on a stop sign
4 = quarts in a gallon
24 = hours in a day
1 = wheel on a unicycle
5 = digits in a zip code
57 = Heinz varieties
11 = players on an American football team
1,000 = words that a picture is worth
29 = days in February in a leap year
64 = squares on a checkerboard
3 = blind mice (see how they run)

APPENDIX 2-E: THREE-WORD WONDERS

Table A2-E.   Three-Word Wonders

Hoover	Queen	Quiver	Pinto	Pinto	Basketball
Truman	King	Holster	Palomino	Mustang	Doghouse
Kennedy	Jack	Sheath	Clydesdale	Jaguar	Football
Sacramento	Triangle	Noon	Scales	Pluto	Bell
Harrisburg	Octagon	Did	Feathers	Mickey	Whitney
Frankfort	Pentagon	Peep	Fur	Minnie	Fulton
Delete	Bloom	Blume	Bilbo	Charlie Buckett	Mohawk
Expunge	Depp	Milne	Gandolf	Willy Wonka	Huron
Erase	Knightly	Dahl	Gollum	Mr. Fox	Appache
Mohawk	Tux	Smog	Tepee	Flea	Elizabeth
Afro	Limo	Chunnel	Hogan	Tapeworm	Victoria
Crew cut	Vet	Motel	Wickiup	Tick	Anne
Manx	Sonnet	He	Dorm	Cup	Red
Persian	Limerick	She	Champ	Green	Grey
Siamese	Haiku	They	Ump	Trap	Timber
Columbus	Luke	Spratt	Heather	Spot	Twist
Hudson	Peter	Nicholson	Rose	Shot	Fagen
Drake	Paul	Knife	Violet	Cakes	Heep

APPENDIX 2-F: HINK PINKS AND
HINKY PINKYS AND HINKETY PINKETYS

1. comical rabbit = a funny bunny
2. obese feline = a fat cat
3. carpet for an insect =
4. paw cover for a young cat =
5. banana-colored man =
6. rose's strength =
7. big town's sympathy =
8. dull crustacean =
9. unique duo =
10. gentle orange peel =
11. adorable salamander =
12. magic formula of the sea =
13. burning pan =
14. large hog =

15. seat for a monarch's skeleton =
16. salmon's hope =
17. grumpy handkerchief =
18. bloody tale =
19. courageous rescue =
20. handbag's spell =
21. bathing time =
22. morning ice not found =
23. smashed head covering =
24. entry way for a wild pig =
25. rodent's home =
26. noisy vapor in sky =
27. nettle's tune =
28. sow's hairpiece =
29. rug for a feline =
30. runner in the snow =
31. large stream's shake =
32. evil preacher =
33. letter found in a canoe =
34. sneaky woman =
35. person who steals steaks =
36. weak escargot =
37. better place to eat =
38. improved correspondence =
39. quiet tramp =
40. five cent cucumber =
41. child's bed =
42. drinking apparatus in Poconos =
43. child's transportation =
44. male plaything =
45. father in a good mood = happy pappy
46. large porker =
47. outstanding film in the '60s =
48. wagers by New York baseball players =
49. raise one's glass at seaside =
50. refuge for black birds =

Our Language Keeps Growing

APPENDIX 3-A: NONSTANDARD WORDS

(Also see William Safire's column in the *New York Times Magazine*, June 29, 2003.)

Here is a brief list of nonstandard words that have recently been added to dictionaries, from *Webster's New World Dictionary* to the *Historical* (Hysterical?) *Dictionary of American Slang*. (It's apparent to me that they're def and phat words!)

barista—a person who makes and serves coffee to the public
frankenfood—genetically modified food
lexies—dictionary writers
scam—con game
swamp angel—mosquito
snorter—a heavy gale
scope out—to look at
boytoy—an attractive man regarded as being a readily compliant companion
kleptocracy—a regime characterized by the theft of its country's natural resources
funplex—an entertainment complex that involves facilities for several sports
def—cool
phat—highly gratifying

Can your students think of more? Several years ago the word "macho" came into our language—it was popularized in a song by the Village People. (I also remember that a muppet poked fun at the "male chauvinist pigs.") Anyway, let your students have fun!

APPENDIX 3-B: FOREIGN WORDS AND PHRASES

Foreign words and phrases are used in many media, and students should learn—and should enjoy learning—some of the more common ones.

ad nauseum—to the point of disgust (Latin)

a la carte—according to the menu (French)

a la mode—in fashion (French)

aloha—hello or goodbye (Hawaiian)

alfresco—outdoors (Italian)

au contraire—on the contrary (French)

au revior—until we meet again (French)

bona fide—in good faith (Latin)

bon jour—good day (French)

bon vivant—lover of good living (French)

bon voyage—have a good trip (French)

carte blanche—full authority (French)

caveat emptor—let the buyer beware (Latin)

cul-de-sac—dead end (French)

double entendre—double meaning (French)

emeritus—retired after long service (Latin)

en masse—in large group (French)

en route—on the way (French)

entourage—those closely associated with a person (French)

esprit de corps—group spirit (French)

et al.—and others (Latin)

et cetera—and so forth (Latin)

eureka—I have found it (Greek)

faux pas—mistake or mistakes (French)

hors d'oeuvre—appetizer (French)

in memoriam—in memory of (Latin)

khaki—olive tan color (Hindi)

malapropos—out of place (French)

mea culpa—my fault (Latin)

modus operandi—manner of working (Latin)

nom de plume—pen name (French)

penchant—strong liking or inclination (French)

prima donna—first lady (Italian)

protégé—one under guidance of another (French)

raconteur—story teller (French)

respondez s'il vous plait (RSVP)—please respond/reply (French)

status quo—the way things are (Latin)

tortilla—round, flat unleavened bread (Spanish)

veranda—large porch (Latin)

vice versa—conversely (Latin)

vis-à-vis—in relation to (French)

wanderlust—passion for traveling (German)

Useful Lists

APPENDIX 4-A: HOMOPHONES

Homophones are words that sound the same but have different meanings and different spellings. Homophones are particularly worthy of attention now that so many people are using spell-checkers. A spell-checker approves any word spelled correctly even though the writer has used an incorrect homophone. There is no substitute for careful proofing! Please note that "definitions" in these lists are purposefully quite brief; they are more cues to differentiate than true definitions. Many of the words are also multi-meaning, for example, "bear" and "bale."

aid (assist)
aide (a helper)

ail (be unwell)
ale (a drink)

air (we breathe it)
heir (male successor)

aisle (path)
I'll (I will)
isle (island)

all (total)
awl (tool)

allowed (permitted)
aloud (not silent)

already (previous)
all ready (all are ready)

altar (in a church)
alter (change)

arc (curved line)
ark (boat)

ascent (climb)
assent (agree)

assistance (help)
assistants (helpers)

ate (consumed)
eight (number)

aye (yes)
eye (organ to see)
I (pronoun)

ball (round object)
bawl (cry)

band (plays)
banned (forbidden)

bare (uncovered)
bear (animal)

base (lower part)
bass (deep tone)

beach (shore)
beech (tree)

beat (defeat)
beet (vegetable)

berth (bunk)
birth (born)

better (superior)
bettor (one who bets)

billed (did bill)
build (construct)

blew (puffed)
blue (color)

board (lumber)
bored (tired of)

bough (of a tree)
bow (of a ship)

brake (stop)
break (destroy)

bridal (of a bride)
bridle (for a horse)

buy (purchase)
by (near)
bye (adieu)

cannon (big gun)
canon (law)

carat (weight of gem)
caret (proofreader's mark)
carrot (vegetable)

cast (actors)
caste (social class)

cell (prison room)
sell (vend)

cellar (basement)
seller (vendor)

cent (penny)
scent (odor)
sent (did send)

cereal (of grain)
serial (of a series)

chased (did chase)

chaste (pure)

chews (masticates)
choose (select)

chilly (cold)
chili (hot pepper)

chord (musical notes)
cord (string)

claws (nails on
    animals feet)
clause (part of a
    sentence)

close (shut)
clothes (clothing)

coarse (rough)
course (school subject)

colonel (military rank)
kernel (of corn)

complement
    (go together)
compliment (praise)

coop (chicken pen)
coupe (car)

council (advising
    group)
counsel (advise)

cue (prompt)
queue (line up)

deer (animal)
dear (greeting;
    loved one)

desert (abandon)
dessert (last course
    of meal)

do (act)
dew (moisture)
due (owed)

dual (two)
duel (formal combat)

ewe (female sheep)
yew (bush)
you (personal
    pronoun)

eyelet (small hole)
islet (small island)

faint (weak)
feint (pretend attack)

fair (honest)
fare (cost of transportation)

feat (accomplishment)
feet (plural of foot)

find (discover)
fined (assessed penalty)

fir (tree)
fur (animal covering)

flair (ability)
flare (flaming signal)

flea (insect)
flee (run away)

flew (in the air)
flu (influenza)

flour (for cooking)
flower (bud of a plant)

for (in favor of)
fore (front part)
four (number)

forth (forward)
fourth (after third)

foul (bad)
fowl (bird)

groan (sound)
grown (mature)

guessed (estimated)
guest (company)

hail (ice; salute)
hale (healthy)

hair (on head)
hare (rabbit)

hall (passage)
haul (carry)

hangar (storage building)
hanger (to hang things on)

heal (make well)
heel (bottom of foot)
he'll (he will)
hear (listen)
here (this place)

heard (listened)
herd (animals)

heed (pay attention)
he'd (he would)

hew (carve, cut)
hue (color)

higher (above)
hire (employ)

him (pronoun)
hymn (religious song)

hoarse (husky voice)
horse (animal)

hole (opening)
whole (complete)

hour (sixty minutes)
our (possessive pronoun)

idle (unoccupied)
idol (god)

in (opposite of out)
inn (hotel)

insight (self-knowledge)
incite (start, set off)

its (possessive pronoun)
it's (it is)

knight (warrior)
night (evening)

knit (with yarn)
nit (louse egg)

knot (tangle)
not (in no way)

lead (metal)
led (guided)

lean (slender)
lien (claim)

leased (rented)
least (smallest)

lessen (make less)
lesson (instruction)

lie (fib)
lye (acid)

load (burden)
lode (vein of ore)

loan (to lend)
lone (single)

made (manufactured)
maid (servant)
mail (send a letter)
male (masculine)

main (most important)
Maine (state)
mane (hair)

mall (place to shop)
maul (to maim)

manner (style)
manor (estate)

meat (beef)
meet (greet)
mete (measure)

medal (award)
meddle (interfere)
mettle (courage)
metal (like iron)

might (may, strength)
mite (small insect)

miner (coal digger)
minor (juvenile)

missed (failed)
mist (fog)

moan (groan)
mown (cut down)

none (not any)
nun (religious sister)

oar (of a boat)
or (conjunction)

ode (poem)
owed (did owe)

one (number)
won (triumphed)

overdo (go to
  extremes)
overdue (past due)

overseas (abroad)
oversees (supervises)

pail (bucket)
pale (ashen)

pair (two of a kind)
pare (peel)
pear (fruit)

passed (went by)
past (former)

peace (serenity)
piece (part)

pedal (ride a bike)
peddle (sell)
petal (flower part)

peer (equal)
pier (dock)

plain (simple)
plane (flat surface)

pleas (plural of plea)
please (to be agreeable)

pole (stick, rod)
poll (vote)

pore (skin gland)
pour (flow freely)
poor (without money)

presents (gifts)
presence (appearance)

principal (chief)
principle (rule)

profit (benefit)
prophet (seer)

rain (precipitation)
reign (royal authority)
rein (harness)

raise (put up)
raze (tear down)
rays (of sun)

read (peruse)
reed (plant)

read (perused)
red (color)

real (genuine)
reel (spool)

rest (relax)
wrest (take from)

right (correct)
rite (ceremony)
write (as a letter)

ring (circular band)
wring (squeeze)

road (street)
rode (traveled)
rowed (used oars)

role (part)
roll (turn over)

root (part of a plant)
route (highway)

rose (flower)
rows (lines)

rote (by memory)
wrote (did write)

rung (step on a ladder)
wrung (squeezed)

sail (travel by boat)
sale (bargain)

scene (setting)
seen (viewed)

scent (smell)
sent (mailed)
cent (penny)

sear (singe)
seer (prophet)

sew (mend)
so (in order that)
sow (plant)

shone (beamed)
shown (exhibited)

side (flank)
sighed (audible breath)

slay (kill)
sleigh (sled)

soar (fly)
sore (hurting)

sole (only)
soul (spirit)

some (part)
sum (total)

son (offspring)
sun (star)

stair (step)
stare (look intently)

stake (post)
steak (meat)

stationary (fixed)
stationery (paper)

steal (rob)
steel (metal)

straight (not crooked)
strait (channel of water)

suite (connected rooms)
sweet (sugary)

tail (animal's end of spine)
tale (story)
taught (did teach)
taut (tight)

tea (drink)
tee (for golf ball)

team (crew)
teem (be full)

tear (cry)
tier (level)

teas (plural of tea)
tease (mock)
tees (plural: holders of golf balls)

their (possessive pronoun)
there (at the place)
they're (they are)

threw (tossed)
through (finished)

throne (king's seat)
thrown (tossed)

tide (ebb and flow)
tied (bound)

to (toward)
too (also)
two (number)

toe (digit on foot)
tow (pull)

told (inform)
tolled (rang)

vain (conceited)
vane (wind indicator)
vein (blood vessel)

vale (valley)
veil (face cover)

waist (middle)
waste (trash)

wait (linger)
weight (heaviness)

ware (item)
wear (have on)
where (what place)

we (pronoun)
wee (small)

weak (not strong)
week (seven days)

weather (climate)
whether (if)

weave (interlace)
we've (we have)

we'd (we would)
weed (plant)

which (what one)
witch (sorceress)

whine (complaining
  sound)
wine (drink)

who's (who is)
whose (possessive of
  who)

your (possessive
  pronoun)
you're (you are)

wood (of a tree)
would (is willing to)

APPENDIX 4-B: HOMOGRAPHS AND HETERONYMS

Homographs are words that are spelled the same but have different meanings and different origins. (Homographs that are also heteronyms—which also have a different pronunciation—are marked with an asterisk.)

arms (limbs)
arms (weapons)

bail (money for
  release)
bail (get water out)

ball (round object)
ball (formal dance)

band (group of
  musicians)
band (thin strip)

bank (mound)
bank (place for money)
bank (land along a
  river)

*bass (low male voice)
bass (kind of fish)

bat (club)
bat (flying animal)
bat (wink)

bear (large animal)
bear (carry)

bill (money owed)
bill (beak)

bit (small piece)
bit (did bite)

blow (hard hit)
blow (send forth
  air)

bluff (cliff)
bluff (fool)

boom (long beam)
boom (deep sound)

bore (make a hole)
bore (make tired)

bound (tied)
bound (obliged)
bound (on the way)

*bow (weapon for
  shooting arrows)
bow (forward part of a
  ship)
bow (greeting)

bowl (deep dish)
bowl (play the game)

bridge (span)
bridge (card game)

brush (for grooming)
brush (bushes)

buck (male deer)
buck (slang for dollar)
buck (avert anything)

can (able to)
can (container)

capital (money)
capital (punishable by
  death)

carp (complain)
carp (kind of fish)

case (condition)
case (container)

chop (cut)
chop (cut of meat)

clip (cut)
clip (fasten)

**close* (shut)
close (near)

**commune* (talk
  intimately)
commune (people
  living together)

**compact* (packed
  together)
compact
  (agreement)

con (swindle)
con (anti)

**console* (cabinet)
console (ease grief)

**content* (all things
  inside)
content (satisfied)

**converse* (talk)
converse (opposite)

count (name
  numbers)
count (nobleman)

counter (in a
  kitchen)
counter (opposite)

cue (signal)
cue (long pool
  stick)

date (day, month,
  and year)
date (sweet fruit)
date (go out with)

**desert* (dry barren
  region)
desert (abandon)

die (stop living)
die (tool)

dock (wharf)
dock (cut some off)

**dove* (pigeon)
dove (did dive)

down (from a higher
  to lower place)
down (soft feathers)

ear (organ of hearing)
ear (part of corn)

**entrance* (going in)
entrance (charm)

fan (to stir up the air)
fan (admirer)

fast (speedy)
fast (go without
  food)

fawn (young deer)
fawn (try to get
  favor)

fell (did fall)
fell (cut down)

felt (did feel)
felt (cloth)

file (drawer; folder)
file (tool to smooth)
file (put away)

fine (high quality)
fine (money paid to
  punish)

firm (solid; hard)
firm (company)

flounder (struggle)
flounder (kind of fish)

fly (insect)
fly (move through the
  air)

forge (blacksmith
  shop)
forge (move ahead)

found (did find)
found (set up;
  establish)

fresh (newly made)
fresh (impudent)

fry (cook in pan)
fry (young fish)

grave (place of burial)
grave (serious)

graze (feed on grass)
graze (touch lightly
  in passing)

grouse (game bird)
grouse (complain)

gum (sticky substance)
gum (around teeth)

hail (pieces of ice that fall)
hail (shout)

hamper (hold back)
hamper (large basket)

haze (mist; smoke)
haze (bully; harass)

hide (conceal)
hide (animal skin)

hold (grasp and keep)
hold (part of a ship)

*intimate (very familiar)
intimate (suggest)

*invalid (disabled person)
invalid (not valid)

jar (container of glass)
jar (rattle; vibrate)

jet (stream of water, steam, or air)
jet (type of airplane)

jig (dance)
jig (fishing lure)

kind (same class)
kind (friendly; helpful)

lap (body part formed when sitting)
lap (drink)
lap (trip around a track)

lash (hit with a whip)
lash (tie or fasten)

*lead (show the way)
lead (metallic element)

lean (stand slanting)
lean (not fat)

leave (go away)
leave (permission)
leave (hiatus)

left (direction)
left (did leave)

lie (fib)
lie (falsehood)
lie (rest)

light (not heavy)
light (not dark)

like (similar to)
like (be pleased with)

limp (lame walk)
limp (not stiff)

line (piece of cord)
line (place fabric inside)
line (straight demarcation)

list (series of words)
list (tilt to one side)
list (enumerate)

*live (exist)
live (having life)

lock (fasten; secure)
lock (curl of hair)

long (elongated)
long (wish for)

loom (frame for weaving)
loom (threaten)

mail (letters)
mail (flexible armor)

maroon (brownish red color)
maroon (leave helpless)

match (stick used to light fired)
match (equal)

meal (food served)
meal (ground grain)

mean (signify; intend)
mean (unkind)
mean (average)

might (past of may)
might (power)

*minute (sixty seconds)
minute (very small)

mole (spot on the skin)
mole (small animal)

mount (high hill)
mount (go up)

nag (scold)
nag (old horse)

net (open-weave
   fabric)
net (remaining money)

nip (pinch)
nip (small drink)

*object (a thing)
object (to protest)

pad (cushion)
pad (walk softly)

pawn (leave as
   security)
pawn (chess piece)

pen (instrument
   for writing)
pen (enclosed yard)

pine (type of evergreen)
pine (yearn or long for)

pitch (throw)
pitch (tar)

pitcher (container for
   liquid)
pitcher (baseball
   player)

poach (hunt illegally)
poach (cook an egg)

pole (long piece of
   wood)
pole (earth's axis)
policy (plan of action)
policy (written
   agreement)

post (support)
post (job or position)

pound (unit of weight)
pound (hit hard again
   and again)
pound (pen)

*present (not absent)
present (gift)
present (introduce)

press (squeeze)
press (force into
   service)

prime (chief)
prime (prepare)

prune (fruit)
prune (cut; trim)

punch (hit)
punch (beverage)

pupil (student)
pupil (part of the eye)

racket (noise)
racket (paddle)

rare (unusual)
rare (not
   cooked much)

rash (hasty)
rash (spots on the skin)
rear (the back part)
rear (bring up)

*record (music disk)
record (write down)

refrain (hold back)
refrain (part repeated)

*refuse (say no)
refuse (waste; trash)

rest (sleep)
rest (what is left)

root (part of a plant)
root (cheer for)

sap (liquid in plant)
sap (weaken)

saw (did see)
saw (tool for cutting)
saw (wise saying)

scale (balance)
scale (on fish
scale (climb)

second (after the first)
second (one-sixtieth
   of a minute)

shed (small shelter)
shed (get rid of)

slug (small slow-
moving animal)
slug (hit hard)

snarl (growl)
snarl (tangle)

snare (type of drum)
snare (trap)

sock (covering for
foot)
sock (hit hard)

*sow (scatter seeds)
sow (female pig)

squash (racquet sport)
squash (press flat)
squash (vegetable)

stable (building
for horses)
stable (steady)

stake (stick or post)
stake (risk or prize)

stalk (stem of plant)
stalk (follow secretly)

stall (place in a stable)
stall (delay)

steep (having a sharp
slope)
steep (soak)

stern (rear part of
a ship)
stern (harsh; strict)

stick (pierce)
stick (thin piece of
wood)
stoop (bend down)
stoop (porch)

story (tale)
story (floor of a
building)

strand (leave helpless)
strand (thread or
string)

strip (narrow piece of
cloth)
strip (remove)

stroke (hit)
stroke (pet; smooth)

tart (sour)
tart (small pie)

*tear (drop of liquid
from the eye)
tear (pull apart)

temple (side of
forehead)
temple (building for
worship)

tend (incline to)
tend (take care of)

tick (sound of a clock)
tick (small insect)

till (plow the land)
till (drawer for money)

tip (end point)
tip (of money for
services)

toast (to raise a
glass)
toast (browned bread
slices)

troll (ugly dwarf)
troll (method of
fishing)

unaffected (not
influenced)
unaffected (innocent)

vault (for valuables or
money)
vault (jump over)

well (satisfactory)
well (hole for water)

will (for distribution
of property)
will (deliberate
intention)

*wind (air in motion)
wind (turn)

*wound (hurt)
wound (wrapped
around)

yard (space around a
house)
yard (thirty-six
inches)

APPENDIX 4-C: WORDS COMMONLY CONFUSED

These are words that sound alike or have other confusingly similar characteristics. They have different meanings, and their misuse can cause amusement.

accent (n)—stress in speech or writing
ascent (n)—going up
assent (v, n)—consent, agreement

accept (v)—to agree or take
except (prep)—leaving out or excluding

access (n)—admittance
excess (n, adj) surplus

adapt (v)—to adjust
adept (adj)—skilled
adopt (v)—to take by choice

affect (v)—to influence
effect (n)—result of a cause

all ready (adj)—completely ready
already (adv)—by this time

all together (pron, adj)—everything in one place
altogether (adv)—entirely

breadth (n)—width
breath (n)—respiration
breathe (v)—to inhale and exhale

cease (v)—to stop
seize (v)—to grasp

coma (n)—unconscious state
comma (n)—a punctuation mark

command (n, v)—an order, to order
commend (v)—to praise

costume (n)—special way of dressing
custom (n)—usual practice

decent (adj)—proper
descent (n)—way down
dissent (n, v)—disagreement

depraved (adj)—morally corrupt
deprived (adj)—taken away from

device (n)—a contrivance gadget
devise (v)—to plan

elapse (v)—to pass
lapse (v)—to become void
relapse (v)—to fall back

elicit (v)—to draw out
illicit (adj)—unlawful

emigrate (v)—to leave a country
immigrate (v)—to enter a country

envelop (v)—to surround
envelope (n)—for a letter

formally (adv)—with rigid ceremony
formerly (adv)—previously

human (adj)—relating to mankind
humane (adv)—kind

later (adj)—more late
latter (adj)—second in a series
    of two

lay (v)—to set something down
lie (v)—to recline

loose (adj)—not tight
lose (v)—not win; misplace

moral (n, adj)—lesson; ethic
morale (n)—mental condition

pasture (n)—grass field
pastor (n)—minister

persecute(v)—to harass or annoy
prosecute (v)—to press for
    punishment

personal (adj)—private
personnel (n)— employed
    people

precede (v)—to go before
proceed (v)—to advance

preposition (n)—a part of speech
proposition (n)—a proposal or
    suggestion

quiet (adj)—not noisy
quit (v)—to stop, give up
quite (adv)—very

recent (adj)—not long ago
resent (v)—to feel indignant

through (prep)—by means of
thorough (adj)—complete

trough (n)—animals drink out
    of it
tough (adj)—rugged

veracious (adj)—honest, truthful
voracious (adj)—very greedy

APPENDIX 4-D: SYNONYMS

Synonyms are words that have *similar* meanings (for no two words are *exactly* the same). There are whole books of synonyms that have clusters of words or phrases, all with similar meanings. The word sets I've asterisked make the point that no two words can mean exactly the same thing. These trios, if used in word analogies, would qualify as "degree" analogies, for at least one of the three words is clearly more intense than the rest. For example, take *alarm—frighten—terrify*: in my mind, a noise or a minor incident can "alarm" or "frighten," but "terrify" is a much stronger connotation. Same thing with "large" and "big" vis-à-vis "enormous."

abrupt—sudden—unplanned

allow—permit—grant

*anger—rage—fury

appreciative—grateful—thankful

ask—question—query

brave—courageous—daring

blunder—error—mistake

carry—hand—lug

close—shut—seal

concept—idea—thought

*continue—persevere—persist

danger—peril—hazard

decrease—lessen—abate

disaster—calamity—catastrophe

during—while—simultaneously

energy—power—strength

error—mistake—fallacy

fat—obese—stout

food—nourishment—grub

form—shape—configuration

donation—gift—present

grasp—hold—clutch

great—grand—large

happy—joyous—elated

have—own—possess

*hate—detest—despise

hurry—rush—accelerate

job—work—vocation

just—fair—right

kind—considerate—helpful

kill—slaughter—murder

*large—big—enormous

last—endure—persist

late—tardy—delayed

marvelous—wonderful—awesome

method—way—manner

near—close by—in the vicinity

noise—uproar—clamor

often—frequently—repeatedly

omit—delete—remove

outlive—survive—outlast

pain—ache—hurt

pair—couple—duo

part—portion—piece

peak—summit—top

play—cavort—romp

praise—acclaim—applaud

prohibit—ban—restrict

put—place—locate

remote—distant—secluded

renew—restore—revive

respect—adore—revere

right—correct—proper

say—articulate—remark

seem—appear—look

sorry—regretful—contrite

*speed—haste—hurry

supply—provide—furnish

surpass—exceed—outstore

tense—taut—rigid

*terrify—frighten—scare

thaw—melt—dissolve

*think—reflect—contemplate

time—period—era

*tiny—small—minute

trial—test—experiment

true—faithful—loyal

turn—revolve—pivot

*ugly—homely—plain

understand—comprehend—see

vacant—empty—unoccupied

value—worth—price

*vast—huge—enormous

walk—stroll—saunter

*want—desire—crave

weak—feeble—frail

work—labor—toil

write—inscribe—record

APPENDIX 4-E: ANTONYMS

Antonyms are words that mean the opposite (or nearly the opposite) of each other. Both synonyms and antonyms are often used in tests and language drills

admit—reject	hire—fire	problem—solution
allow—prevent	hot—cold	profit—loss
amateur—professional	idle—active	raise—lower
ascend—descend	in—out	raw—cooked
attract—repel	jolly—morose	regret—rejoice
backward—forward	joy—sadness	relax—tighten
better—worse	keep—lose	revenge—forgiveness
big—little	kind—cruel	rigid—flexible
birth—death	less—more	sad—happy
blunt—sharp	level—uneven	satisfy—displease
boastful—modesty	long—short	secluded—public
busy—idle	male—female	shade—light
buy—sell	man—woman	sharp—dull
chilly—warm	many—few	shy—bold
compliment–insult	mix—separate	silent—loud
cry—laugh	move—stay	slave—master
damage—mend	obese—gaunt	slow—fast
distant—adjacent	obvious—covert	soak—dry
doubt—trust	offend—please	sour—sweet
drunk—sober	offer—refuse	spend—save
exceptional—common	one—many	stay—leave
fancy—plain	pain—pleasure	steal—provide
fast—slow	panic—calm	still—moving
free—capture	partial—total	strength—weakness
freeze—melt	permit—refuse	suspect—trust
friend—foe	pessimistic—optimistic	teach—learn
ground—sky	play—work	thaw—freeze
head—foot	powerful—puny	thin—thick
healthy—ailing	preceding—following	
hill—valley	present—absent	

Antonyms are often easier and make better pairs than synonyms—for example, friend and foe as opposed to foe and adversary.

APPENDIX 4-F: METAPHORS

A metaphor is a figure of speech in which a word or phrase literally denoting one kind of object or idea is used in place of another to suggest a likeness or analogy between them. It compares two unlike things but does not use the words "like" or "as." Below are a number of examples:

Jealousy is a green-eyed monster.
That car is an old dinosaur.
Her porcelain skin is flawless.
He is faster than a streak of lightening.
Use kid gloves when handling this.
The mountain of paperwork seemed to grow.
She is the shining star in his dark, dreary life.
His bark is worse than his bite.
His new car turned out to be a lemon.
The police were determined to get to the bottom of the mystery.
I'm a real chicken when it comes to getting an injection.
When I was lost in the woods, the branches of the trees became hands reaching out to grab me.
His stomach was a bottomless pit.

APPENDIX 4-G. SIMILES

A simile uses "like" or "as" to draw a comparison. These figures of speech are often clichés.

Alyssa's skin was as white as new fallen snow.
Bob's class kept him as busy as a beaver.
The squirrel was squashed as flat as a pancake.
Steven drinks like a fish.
Jose runs like the wind.
Barry is as meek as a lamb.
Maureen cried like a baby.
Alex is as strong as an ox.
Nathaniel is as sly as a fox.

APPENDIX 4-H: IDIOMATIC EXPRESSIONS

An idiomatic expression is peculiar to itself either grammatically or in having a meaning that cannot be derived from the conjoined meanings of its elements. Students who are learning the English language find idiomatic expressions particularly troublesome. It's a good idea to teach the expressions just as you would teach single vocabulary words.

Bill put the old paper in the *circular file*.
Skippy and Camille *don't see eye to eye* on everything.
It *cost an arm and leg* to get the VCR fixed.
Nobody likes a *backseat driver*.
We need to *clear the air*.
I got *cold feet* when it was my turn to speak.
Jody hardly *cracked a book* all weekend.
His *eyes popped out* when he saw the bill.
Money *burns a whole in his pocket*.
We have a *fat chance* of getting done in time.
The party was *for the birds*.
I'd *give my right arm* to own a plane.
Debbie saw the *writing on the wall*.
Jennifer's new car *hugged the road*.
We're all *in the same boat*.
Adam kept his *nose in a book* all afternoon.
She's *not playing with a full deck*.
Lunch was *on the house*.
Ryan *got up on the wrong side of the bed*.
Lisa *took the rap* for the others.
He didn't *know the ropes*.
Keep it *under your hat*.
Biff has a *green thumb*.

APPENDIX 4-I: GREEK AND LATIN ROOTS

The Greek and Latin word parts are of high utility in terms of time-cost, for they are efficient. Learning a single root can lead to many new words, either brand new, or solidifying and reinforcing. Following are the Latin and Greek roots covered in chapter 7, with a few more added in.

Word Part/Origin	Meaning	Example(s)
a, abs, ab (L)	away	abstract, absent
act (L)	do	action, actor, enact
aero (G)	air	aerobics, aerodynamics, aeronautics
agri (L)	field	agriculture, agrarian
alt (L)	high	altitude, alto
ambul (L)	walk	ambulance, amble, somnambulant
andr (G)	man	androgynous, android
art (L)	skill	artisan, artist, artifact
belli (L)	war	belligerent, bellicose, rebellion
biblio (G)	book	bibliography, bible
brev (L)	short	abbreviation, brevity
cal (L)	hot	calorie, caldron, scald
cap (L)	head	caption, capital, decapitate
cardi (G)	heart	cardiologist, cardiac, cardiogram
centr (L)	center	eccentric, egocentric, centrifugal
chron (G)	time	chronological, anachronism
cline (L)	to lean	incline, decline, disinclination
cred (L)	believe	credit, incredible, incredulous
cycl (G)	circle, ring	bicycle, tricycle, cycle, cyclone
dent (L)	tooth	dentist, trident, indent
dict (L)	say, speak	contradict, dictation
dox (G)	belief	orthodox, unorthodox
duc (L)	lead	duct, induct, conduct
fac (L)	do, make	manufacture, facsimile
fer (L)	carry	reference, transfer
fid (L)	faith	fidelity, infidelity, confidence
flex (L)	bend	reflex, flexible, flexor
funct (G)	perform	function, malfunction, dysfunctional
gen (G)	birth, race	generate, genocide, progeny
gram (G)	letter, written	telegram, diagram, grammar
graph (G)	write	autograph, telegraph, phonograph
homo (L)	man	homicide, homage, hombre
hum (L)	ground	exhume, inhume
hydr (G)	water	hydrant, dehydrated
init (L)	beginning	initiate, initiative, initial
ject (L)	throw	project, inject, trajectory
kine (L)	movement	kinetic, hyperkinesis
laps (L)	slip	elapse, collapse, relapse
loc (L)	place	locate, location, dislocate
loqu (L)	speak	eloquence, eloquent

luc (L)	light	lucid, translucent
lust (L)	shine	luster, lackluster, illustrious
man (L)	hand	manacle, manual, manuscript
mania (G)	madness	maniac, maniacal, pyromania
migr (L)	change, move	migrate, immigrate, migratory
morph (G)	shape	amorphous, polymorphous
mort (L)	death	mortal, immortal, mortgage
narr (L)	tell	narrator, narrative
neg (L)	no	negative, renege
neuro (G)	nerve	neurology, neurosurgery
numer (L)	number	numeral, numerous, enumerate
onym (G)	name	pseudonym, homonym, synonym
ortho (G)	straight, right	orthodox, orthodontist
path (G)	to feel, hurt	pathetic, pathology
ped (L)	foot	pedal, pedestrian, pseudopod
phil (G)	love	philosophy, philanthropy, Philadelphia
port (L)	carry	portage, import, transport
psych (G)	mind, soul	psyche, psychology, psychopath
quest (L)	ask, seek	request, inquest, quest
reg (L)	guide, rule	regal, regulate, regime
rupt (L)	break	interrupt, rupture, erupt
san (L)	health	sanitary, insane, sanguine
sanct (G)	holy	sanctify, sanctuary
soph (G)	wise	sophisticated, philosopher
struct (L)	build	construct, construction, structure
tain (L)	hold	retain, pertain, retainer
therm (G)	heat	thermometer, thermal, thermostat
trans (L)	across, beyond	transport, transatlantic, transact
trib (L)	give	contribute, attribute
urb (L)	city	urban, urbane, suburb
vac (L)	empty	vacate, vacuum, vacation
vict (L)	conquer	victory, victim, conviction
vid (L)	see	video, provide, evidence
xen (G)	*foreign*	xenophobic, xenophobia

They Said It

Proverbs are common, wise, or thoughtful sayings that are short and often applicable to different situations. Every culture and language has its own.

Don't count your chickens until they're hatched.
A bird in the hand is worth two in the bush.
You can lead a horse to water, but you can't make it drink.
The early bird catches the worm.
Curiosity killed the cat.
You can't teach an old dog new tricks.
Don't cry over spilt milk.
Too many cooks spoil the broth.
You can't have your cake and eat it too.
An apple a day keeps the doctor away.
All that glitters is not gold.
Early to bed, early to rise, makes a man healthy, wealthy, and wise.
A rolling stone gathers no moss.
Make hay while the sun shines.
Every cloud has a silver lining.
Leave no stone unturned.
The grass always looks greener on the other side of the fence.
Still waters run deep.
If you can't beat them, join them.
Familiarity breeds contempt.
Absence makes the heart grow fonder.
Do unto others as you would have them do unto you.

If the shoe fits, wear it.
People who live in glass houses shouldn't throw stones.
The pen is mightier than the sword.
Necessity is the mother of invention.
Haste makes waste.
Look before you leap.
Beggars can't be choosers.
Two heads are better than one.
Many hands make light work.
Fool me once, shame on you; fool me twice, shame on me.
Strike while the iron is hot.
Where there's smoke, there's fire.
Out of the frying pan and into the fire.
A watched pot never boils.
This is the first day of the rest of your life.
Waste not, want not.
A quitter never wins, and a winner never quits.
In the land of the blind, the one-eyed man is king.
Sticks and stones can break my bones, but names can never hurt me.
A picture is worth a thousand words.

APPENDIX 5-B: WRITERLY QUOTES

"One must be drenched in words, literally soaked in them, to have the right ones form themselves into the proper pattern at the right moment."
—*Hart Crane*

"The ideal view for daily writing, hour on hour, is the blank brick wall of a cold-storage warehouse. Failing this, a stretch of sky will do, cloudless if possible."
—*Edna Ferber*

"It is not pathetic passages that make us shed our best tears, but the miracle of a word in the right place."
—*Jean Cocteau*

"Nothing you write, if you hope to be any good, will ever come out as you had first hoped."
—*Lillian Hellman*

"Standing by words in the classroom means exploring words for today—for the children and their needs—today. We must help children come to words today—in awe and in love—not in obligation for some committee's business plan for tomorrow."
—*Susan Ohanian*

"Writing is the hardest way of earning a living, with the possible exception of wrestling alligators."
—*Olin Miller*

"The sinister thing about writing is that it starts off seeming so easy and ends up being so hard."
—*L. Rust Mills*

"Asking a working writer what he thinks about critics is like asking a lamppost what it feels about dogs."
—*John Osborne*

"Adam was the only man who, when he said a good thing, knew that nobody had said it before him."
—*Mark Twain*

"Nothing comes easily. My work smells of sweat."
—*Eric Hoffer*

"There are three rules for writing a novel. Unfortunately, no one knows what they are."
—*Somerset Maugham*

"Novel: a short story padded."
—*Ambrose Bierce*

"Some things can only be said in fiction, but that doesn't mean they aren't true."
—*Aaron Latham*

"I suppose I am a born novelist, for the things I imagine are more vital and vivid to me than the things I remember."
—*Ellen Glasgow*

"When I stepped from hard manual work to writing, I just stepped from one kind of hard work to another."
—*Sean O'Casey*

APPENDIX 5-C: STUDENTS' ADAGES

A first grade teacher had twenty-six students in her class. She presented each child in her classroom the beginning of a well-known proverb and asked them all to come up with the remainder of the proverb. It is hard to believe that these adages were actually done by first graders.

1. Happy is the bride who. . . gets all the presents.
2. Where there is smoke there's . . . pollution.

3. An idle mind . . . is the best way to relax.
4. Love all, trust . . . me.
5. You can't teach an old dog . . . math.
6. Don't bite the hand that . . . looks dirty.
7. Don't change horses . . . until they stop running.
8. A bird in the hand . . . is going to poop on you.
9. When the blind lead the blind . . . get out of the way.
10. Children should be seen and not . . . spanked or grounded.
11. Don't put off until tomorrow what . . . you put on to go to bed.
12. Twos company, three's . . . the musketeers.
13 A penny saved is . . . not much.
14. Better late than . . . pregnant.

APPENDIX 5-D: BAD ANALOGIES

Here are some mostly unfortunate but hilarious analogies found in high school students' essays. These came to me as email attachments several years ago. I was not able to find the original sources.

Her face was a perfect oval, like a circle that had its two other sides gently compressed by a Thigh Master.
His thoughts tumbled in his head, making and breaking alliances like underpants in a dryer without Cling Free.
The little boat gently drifted across the pond exactly the way a bowling ball wouldn't.
The whole scene had an eerie, surreal quality like when you're on vacation in another city and *Jeopardy* comes on at 7:00 p.m. instead of 7:30 p.m.
Her eyes were like two brown circles with big black dots in the center.
Her vocabulary was as bad as, like, whatever.
He was as tall as a six-foot-three-inch tree.
The politician was gone but unnoticed, like the period after the Dr. on a Dr Pepper can.
They lived in a typical suburban neighborhood with picket fences that resembled Nancy Kerrigan's teeth.
He fell for her like his heart was a mob informant and she was the East River.
The young fighter had a hungry look, the kind you get from not eating for a while.
Not the metaphorical lame duck, either, but a real duck that was actually lame. Maybe from stepping on a land mine or something.

The dandelion swayed in the gentle breeze like an oscillating electric fan set on medium.

When she spoke, he thought he heard bells, as if she were a garbage truck backing up.

Her eyes were like limpid pools, only they had forgotten to put in any pH cleaner.

APPENDIX 5-E: DANNY OZARK

Worth Misremembering

Yogi Berra was not the sole master of the malapropism. Here are some words of wisdom from former Philadelphia Phillies manager Danny Ozark:

1. "I've got a great repertoire with my players."
2. "Even Napoleon had his Watergate."
3. "It is beyond my apprehension."
4. "His limitations are limitless."
5. "He and I have our indifferences."
6. "How is our morale? Morality at this point isn't a factor."
7. "It really sent a twinkle up my spine" (after an ovation by Phillies fans).

APPENDIX 5-F: OUR INCREDIBLE LANGUAGE

When the English tongue we speak,
Why is "break" not rhymed with "freak"?
Will you tell me why it's true,
We say "sew" but likewise "few"?
And the maker of a verse
Cannot rhyme his "horse" with "worse."
"Beard" sounds not the same as "heard,"
"Cord" is different from "word."
"Cow" is "cow," but "low" is "low,"
"Shoe" is never rhymed with "roe."
Think of "hose" and "dose" and "lose,"
And think of "goose" and yet of "choose."
Think of "comb" and "tomb" and "bomb,"
"Doll" and "roll" and "home" and "come."
And since "pay" is rhymed with "say,"
Why not "paid" and "said," I pray?
We have "blood" and "food" and "good,"
"Mould" is not pronounced like "could."

Wherefore "done" but "gone" and "lone"?
Is there any reason known?
And, in short, it seems to me
Sounds and letters disagree

—Anonymous

References

Afflerbach, P., Pearson, P. D., & Paris, S. (2008). Clarifying differences between reading skills and reading strategies. *The Reading Teacher*, 61, 364–373.

Allen, J. (1999). *Words, words, words: Teaching vocabulary in grades 4–12*. Portland, ME: Stenhouse.

Allen, J. (2007). *Inside words: Tools for teaching academic vocabulary in grades 4–12*. Portland, ME: Stenhouse.

Armbruster, B. B., Lehr, F., & Osborn, J. (2001). *Put reading first: The research building blocks for teaching children to read*. Washington, DC: Center for Improvement of Early Reading Achievement.

Baker, S., Simmons, D., & Kameenui, E. (1995). *Vocabulary acquisition for diverse learners*. Technical Report 13. Eugene: University of Oregon.

Bannon, R. E., Fisher, P., Pozzi, L., & Wessel, D. (1990). Effective definitions for word learning. *Journal of Reading*, 34, 301–302.

Barr, R., Kamil, M. L., Mosenthal, P. B., & Pearson, P. D. (Eds.). (1991). *Handbook of reading research* (Vol. 2). White Plains, NY: Longman.

Barr, R. C., & Johnson, B. (1990). *Teaching reading in elementary classrooms*. White Plains, NY: Longman.

Baumann, J., & Kameenui, E. (1991). Research on vocabulary instruction: Ode to Voltaire. In J. Flood, J. Jensen, D. Lapp, & J. Squire (Eds.), *Handbook of research on teaching the English language arts* (pp. 604–632). New York: Macmillan.

Bear, D., Invernizzi, M., Templeton, S., & Johnson, F. (2007). *Words their way: Word study for phonics, vocabulary, and spelling instruction* (4th ed.). Columbus, OH: Merrill/Prentice Hall.

Beck, I., McCaslin, M., & McKeown, M. (1980). *The rationale and design of a program to teach vocabulary to fourth-grade students*. Pittsburgh: University of Pittsburgh, Learning Research and Development Center.

Beck, I., & McKeown, M. (1983). Learning words well: A program to enhance vocabulary and comprehension. *The Reading Teacher*, 36, 622–625.

Beck, I., & McKeown, M. (1991). Conditions of vocabulary acquisition. In R. Barr, M. Kamil, P. Mosenthal, & P. Pearson (Eds.), *Handbook of reading research* (Vol. 2, pp. 787–814). New York: Longman.

Beck, I., & McKeown, M. (2003, May). Promoting vocabulary development in the early grades. Paper presented at the International Reading Association Conference, Orlando, FL.

Beck, I., McKeown, M., & Kucan, I. (2002). *Bringing words to life: Robust vocabulary instruction*. New York: Guilford.

Beers, K. (2003). *When kids can't read: What teachers can do*. Portsmouth, NH: Heinemann.

Berg, D. (1993). *A guide to the Oxford English dictionary*. Oxford, UK: Oxford University Press.

Blachowicz, C. (1986). Making connections: Alternatives to the vocabulary notebook. *Journal of Reading*, 2, 643–649.

Blachowicz, C. (1993). C2QU: Modeling context use in the classroom. *The Reading Teacher*, 47, 268–269.

Blachowicz, C., & Fisher, P. (2010). *Teaching vocabulary in all classrooms* (4th ed.). Boston: Allyn & Bacon.

Blachowicz, C., Fisher, P., Costa, M., & Pozzi, L. (1993). Researching vocabulary learning in middle school cooperative reading groups: A teacher-researcher collaboration. Paper presented at the Tenth Great Lakes Regional Reading Conference, Chicago.

Cooter, R. (1990). *The teacher's guide to reading tests*. Scottsdale, AZ: Gorsuch.

Cunningham, P. M. (1995). *Phonics they use: Words for reading and writing* (2nd ed.). New York: HarperCollins.

Dana, C., & Rodriquez, M. (1992). TOAST: A system to study vocabulary. *Reading Research and Instruction*, 31(4), 78–84.

Daniels, H. (2002). *Literature circles: Voice and choice in book clubs and reading groups* (2nd ed.). Portland, ME: Stenhouse.

Davey, B. (1983). Think-aloud: Modeling the cognitive process of reading comprehension. *Journal of Reading*, 27, 44–47.

Fisher, D., & Frey, N. (2007a). Implementing a schoolwide literacy framework: Improving achievement in an urban elementary school. *The Reading Teacher*, 61(1), 32–43.

Fisher, D., & Frey, N. (2007b). A tale of two middle schools: The difference in structure and instruction. *Journal of Adolescent and Adult Literacy*, 51(3), 204–212.

Fisher, D., & Frey, N. (2008a). *Better learning through structured teaching: A framework for the gradual release of responsibility*. Alexandria, VA: Association for Curriculum and Staff Development.

Fisher, D., & Frey, N. (2008b). *Word wise and content rich, grades 7–12: Five essential steps to teaching academic literacy*. Portsmouth, NH: Heinemann.

Flanigan, K., & Greenwood, S. C. (2007). Effective content vocabulary instruction in the middle: Matching students, purposes, words, and strategies. *Journal of Adolescent and Adult Literacy*, 51(3), 226–238.

Flower, L., & Hayes, J. (1994). A cognitive process theory of writing. In R. B. Ruddell, M. R. Ruddell, & H. Singer (Eds.), *Theoretical models and processes of reading* (4th ed., pp. 928–950). Newark, DE: International Reading Association.

Frayer, D. A., Frederick, W., & Klausmeier, J. (1969). *A schema for testing the level of concept mastery*. Working Paper 16. Madison: University of Wisconsin.

Fry, E., Kress, J., & Fountoukidis, D. L. (2000). *The reading teacher's book of lists* (4th ed.). Paramus, NJ: Prentice Hall.

Graves, M. F., Juel, C., & Graves, B. B. (2004). *Teaching reading in the 21st century* (3rd ed.). Boston: Allyn & Bacon.

Greenwood, S. C. (2003). *On equal terms: How to make the most of learning contracts in grades 4–9*. Portsmouth, NH: Heinemann.

Greenwood, S. C. (in press). Content area readers: Helping middle level students become word aware (and enjoy it!). *The Clearinghouse*.

Greenwood, S. C., & Flanigan, K. (2007). Overlapping vocabulary and comprehension: Context clues complement semantic gradients. *The Reading Teacher*, 61(3) 249–254.

Haggard, M. (1982). The vocabulary self-collection strategy: An active approach to word learning. *Journal of Reading*, 26, 203–207.

Harmon, J. M., & Hedrick, W. B. (2002). Zooming in and zooming out: Enhancing vocabulary and conceptual learning in social studies. *The Reading Teacher*, 54(2), 155–159.

Harper, C., & deJong, E. (2004). Misconceptions about teaching English language learners. *Journal of Adolescent and Adult Literacy*, 48(2), 152–162.

Harris, A., & Sipay, E. (1990). *How to increase reading ability*. New York: Longman.

Harvey, S., & Goudvis, A. (2006). *Strategies that work* (2nd ed.). Portland, ME: Stenhouse.

Huffbenkoski, K., & Greenwood, S. C. (1995). The use of analogy instruction with developing readers. *The Reading Teacher*, 48(5), 16–19.

Johnson, D. D. (2001). *Vocabulary in the elementary and middle school*. Needham Heights, MA: Allyn & Bacon.

Johnson, D. D., & Pearson, P. D. (1978). *Teaching reading vocabulary*. New York: Holt, Rinehart, and Winston.

Johnston, F., Invernizzi, M., Bear, D. R., & Templeton, S. (2009). *Words their way: Word sorts for syllables and affixes spellers*. Boston: Allyn & Bacon/Pearson.

Johnston, P. H. (2004). *Choice words: How our language affects children's learning*. Portland, ME: Stenhouse.

Lane, B. (1993). *After the end: Teaching and learning creative revision*. Portsmouth, NH: Heinemann.

Lane, B. (1999). *Reviser's toolbox*. Shoreham, UT: Discover Writing Press.

Manzo, A., & Manzo, J. U. (1990). *Content area reading: A heuristic approach*. Columbus, OH: Merrill.

McGinley, W., & Denner, P. (1987). Story impressions: A prereading/writing activity. *Journal of Reading*, 31(3), 248–253.

McKenna, M. C., & Kear, D. J. (1990). Measuring attitude toward reading: A new tool for teachers. *The Reading Teacher*, 43, 626–639.

McKeown, M. (1985). The acquisition of word meaning from content by children of high and low ability. *Reading Research Quarterly*, 20, 482–496.

McKeown, M. (1990). Making dictionary definitions more effective. Paper presented at the American Educational Research Association Annual Convention, Boston, MA.

McKeown, M., & Beck, I. (1991). Direct and rich vocabulary instruction. In J. Baumann and E. Kameenui (Eds.). *Vocabulary Instruction: Research to Practice* (pp. 13–27). New York: Guilford.

Mohr, K. A. (2004). English and accelerate language: A call to ------- for reading teachers. *The Reading Teacher*. 58 (12), 18–26.

Nagy, W. (1988). *Teaching vocabulary to improve reading comprehension*. Newark, DE: International Reading Association.

National Endowment for the Arts. (2007). *To Read or not to read: A question of national consequence*. Washington, DC: Author.

National Reading Panel. (2000). *Report of the National Reading Panel: Teaching children to read*. Washington, DC: National Institute of Child Health and Human Development.

Ogle, D. (1986). K-W-L: A teaching model that develops active reading of expository text. *The Reading Teacher*, 39, 564–70.

Ohanion, S. (2002). *The great word catalogue*. Portsmouth, NH: Heinemann.

Palinscar, A. S., & Brown, A. L. (1984). Reciprocal teaching of comprehension: Fostering comprehension and monitoring activities. *Cognition and Instruction*, 1, 117–175.

Pearson, P. D., & Gallagher, M. G. (1983). The instruction of reading comprehension. *Contemporary Educational Psychology*, 8, 317–344.

Pearson, P. D., & Johnson, D. D. (1984). *Teaching reading comprehension*. New York: Holt, Rinehart, and Winston.

Piper, T. (1993). *And then there were two: Children and second language learning*. Markham, Ontario: Pippin.

Pittelman, S., Heimlich, J., Berglund, R., & French, M. (1991). *Semantic feature analysis: Classroom applications*. Newark, DE: International Reading Association.

Popham, J. (2004). Classroom assessment: What teachers need to know (2nd ed.). Boston: Allyn & Bacon.

Readance, J., Bean, J., & Baldwin, R. (1989). *Content area reading: An integrated approach*. Dubuque, IA: Kendall/Hunt.

Ruddell, M. R., & Shearer, B. A. (2002). "Extraordinary," "tremendous," "exhilarating," "magnificent": Middle school at-risk students become avid word learners with the vocabulary self-collection strategy (VSS). *Journal of Adolescent and Adult Literacy*, 45(5), 352–363.

Safire, W. (2003, June 29). Sexy lexies: Swat that swamp angel, boytoy. *New York Times Magazine*, 18.

Scholfield, P. (1982). Using the English dictionary for comprehension. *TESOL Quarterly*, 16, 185–194.

Schwartz, R., & Raphael, T. (1985). Concept of definition: A key to improving students' vocabulary. *The Reading Teacher*, 39, 198–205.

Snow, C., Burns, S., & Griffin, P. (Eds.). (1998). *Preventing reading difficulties in young children*. Washington, DC: National Academy Press.

Spandel, V. (2004). Creating writers through six trait writing assessment and instruction (4th ed.). Boston: Allyn & Bacon.

Spandel, V., & Stiggins, R. (1997). *Creating writers*. New York: Longman.

Staab, C. (1991). Classroom organization: Thematic centers revisited. *Language Arts*, 68(2), 99–108.

Stahl, S. (1985). To teach a word well: A framework for vocabulary instruction. *Reading World*, 24(3), 16–27.

Stahl, S. (1999). Why innovations come and go: The case of whole language. *Educational Researcher*, 28, 13–22.

Stanovich, K. (1986). Matthew effects in reading: Some consequences of individual difference in the acquisition of reading. *Reading Research Quarterly*, 21, 360–407.

Tierney, R., Readance, J., & Dishner, E. (1985). *Reading strategies and practices: A compendium* (2nd ed.). Newton, MA: Allyn & Bacon.

Trelease, J. (1995). *The new read-aloud handbook* (4th ed.). New York: Penguin.

Unrau, N., & Schlackman, J. (2006). Motivation and its relationship with reading achievement in an urban middle school. *Journal of Educational Research*, 100(2), 81–101.

Vacca, R. T., & Vacca, J. (2001). *Content area reading: Literacy and learning across the curriculum* (7th ed.). New York: Allyn & Bacon.

Walberg, H. (1984). Families as partners in educational productivity. *Phi Delta Kappan*, 65, 397–400.

Welker, W. (1987). Going from typical to technical meaning. *Journal of Reading*, 31, 275–276.

Wood, K. D. (2001). *Literacy strategies across the subject areas*. Boston: Allyn & Bacon.

Woolridge, S. (1996). Poemcrazy: Freeing your life with words. In J. Parker-Webster & L. Van Horn (2000) Tickets to the theatre: Opening the curtain on a dialogue with words. *Voices from the Middle*, 7(4), 9.

LITERATURE CITED

Berendt, John. (1994). *Midnight in the garden of good and evil*. New York: Random House.

Bunting, E. (1991). *Fly away home*. New York: Clarion Books.

Capote, T. (1965). *In cold blood*. New York: Random House.

Cleary, B. (1984). *Dear Mr. Henshaw*. New York: Morrow.

Cole, J. Magic schoolbus (series). New York: Scholastic.

Fritz, J. (1976). *What's the big idea, Ben Franklin?* New York: Coward McCann.

Gaarder, J. (1996). *The solitaire mystery.* New York: Berkley.

George, J. C. (1973). *Julie of the wolves.* New York: Harper.

Golding, W. (1953). *Lord of the flies.* New York: Perigree.

Gwynne, F. (1970). *The king who rained.* New York: Simon and Schuster.

Gwynne, F. (1976). *A chocolate moose for dinner.* New York: Half Moon Books.

Lee, H. (1960). *To kill a mockingbird.* Boston: Little, Brown.

O'Dell, Scott. (1960). *Island of the blue dolphins.* Boston: Houghton Mifflin.

Osborne, M. P. Magic tree house (series). New York: Random House.

Osborne, M. P. (1989). The face in the pool: The story of Echo and Narcissus. *Favorite Greek Myths.* New York: Scholastic.

Parish, P., & Parish, H. Amelia Bedelia (series). New York: Greenwillow Books.

Paulson, G. (1996). *Hatchet.* Boston: Houghton Mifflin.

Speare, E. G. (1983). *The sign of the beaver.* Boston: Houghton Mifflin.

Wallenchensky, D., & Wallace, I. (1975). *The people's almanac.* New York: Doubleday.

Wells, H. G. (1988). *The time machine.* New York: Tom Doherty Associates.

White, E. B. (1952). *Charlotte's web.* New York: Harper.

Index

Cooper, David, 41
core books, 43–46
corruptions, 140
Crane, Hart, 206
criterion-referenced tests, 163
C(2)QU, 68–70
curriculum teaching, 166
cut scores, 163

definitional approaches, 5–6
dictionaries, 126–35; of affixes, 115;
    for grade level, 134; misuse of, 4;
    parts of, 131; types of, 127; use of,
    127–28; when to use, 128–30
direct instruction, 35–38; and
    independent reading, 75; in spelling,
    118–19; time for, 22

Einstein, Albert, 161
Eliminate Words, 107
emotional development, of middle level
    learners, 9
English-language learners (ELLs): cored
    books for, 43; oral cloze for, 54;
    vocabulary instruction for, 25–29
Epictetus, 109
eponyms, 142–43
etymology, 120–21; Greek and Latin
    roots, 202–4
exercises, 4–5
expectations, and ELLs, 28–29
explicit words, 100

Ferber, Edna, 206
Find the Country, 179
Fletcher, Ralph, 91
foreign words/phrases, 185
formative assessment, 162, 167–70
Frayer Model, 16, 76–78, *77*

games. *See* word games
general words, 99, *99*
Gill, Tom, 34
gist clues, 50
Glasgow, Ellen, 207

glossaries, 135
gradual release of responsibility, 18–19
graphic organizers: for narrative text,
    58–59; for new meanings, 81–83, *83*;
    pre and post, 167–68
Greek roots, 202–4
Guess My Word, 104
guide words, 130
Gwynne, Fred, 139

Hellman, Lillian, 206
heteronyms, 192–96
high-stakes tests, 163
hink pinks, 5–6, 141–42, 182–83
Hoffer, Eric, 206
homographs, 146–48, 192–96
homophones, 125, 146–48, 186–92
How Well Do I Know?, 102, *103*
hypernyms, 99
hyponyms, 99

identity development, of middle level
    learners, 9
idioms, 139, 149, 202; ELLs and, 27
illustrated words/phrases, 152–53
imponderables, 158–59
independence, continuum of, 16–17, *17*
independent reading, 11, 35; with cored
    books, 45–46; and direct instruction,
    75; ELLs and, 26; importance of, 41;
    time for, 20
indirect instruction, 32–35
informational text, 39–70
initialisms, 145–46
intelligent guess strategy, 88–89, *89*
italics, 135
item teaching, 166
IT FITS, 86–87, *87*

Johnson, Samuel, 127
Joubert, Antoine, 15

knowledge rating, 66, *66*
known words, new meanings for, 79–89
K-W-L, vocabulary-focused, 85–86

About the Author

Scott C. Greenwood has served as a secondary English teacher, a middle school developmental reading teacher, an elementary reading specialist, and a K–12 supervisor of language arts. He is now associate professor of literacy at West Chester University.

Breinigsville, PA USA
05 November 2010
248722BV00001B/4/P